Mark *for* Young People

Mark *for* Young People

CATE DAVIS

RESOURCE *Publications* · Eugene, Oregon

MARK FOR YOUNG PEOPLE

Growing Roots

Copyright © 2025 Cate Davis. All rights reserved. Except for brief quotations in critical publications or reviews, no part of this book may be reproduced in any manner without prior written permission from the publisher. Write: Permissions, Wipf and Stock Publishers, 199 W. 8th Ave., Suite 3, Eugene, OR 97401.

Resource Publications
An Imprint of Wipf and Stock Publishers
199 W. 8th Ave., Suite 3
Eugene, OR 97401

www.wipfandstock.com

PAPERBACK ISBN: 979-8-3852-4416-4
HARDCOVER ISBN: 979-8-3852-4417-1
EBOOK ISBN: 979-8-3852-4418-8

10/21/25

All Scripture quotations, unless otherwise indicated, are taken from the Holy Bible, New International Version®, NIV®. Copyright ©1973, 1978, 1984, 2011 by Biblica, Inc.™ Used by permission of Zondervan. All rights reserved worldwide. www.zondervan.com The "NIV" and "New International Version" are trademarks registered in the United States Patent and Trademark Office by Biblica, Inc.™

Scripture quotations marked NLT are taken from the *Holy Bible*, New Living Translation, copyright © 1996, 2004, 2015 by Tyndale House Foundation. Used by permission of Tyndale House Publishers, Inc., Carol Stream, Illinois 60188. All rights reserved.

Scripture quotations marked MSG are taken from *THE MESSAGE*, copyright © 1993, 2002, 2018 by Eugene H. Peterson. Used by permission of NavPress. All rights reserved. Represented by Tyndale House Publishers, Inc.

Scripture quotations marked NLV are taken from the *New Life Version*, copyright © 1969 and 2003. Used by permission of Barbour Publishing, Inc., Uhrichsville, Ohio 44683. All rights reserved.

Scripture quotations marked (ESV) are from the ESV® Bible (The Holy Bible, English Standard Version®), © 2001 by Crossway, a publishing ministry of Good News Publishers. ESV Text Edition: 2025. The ESV text may not be quoted in any publication made available to the public by a Creative Commons license. The ESV may not be translated in whole or in part into any other language. Used by permission. All rights reserved.

For Sarah, Makayla, and Milly.
Beloved daughters of the King,
crowned with glory and honor.

Contents

Series Preface | ix
Introduction to the Gospel of Mark | xiii

Day 1	The Good News	1
Day 2	Jesus' Baptism	6
Day 3	In the Wilderness	10
Day 4	The Kingdom of God	14
Day 5	The Authority of Jesus	18
Day 6	The Man with Leprosy	22
Day 7	The Paralyzed Man	26
Day 8	Jesus Welcomes Sinners	30
Day 9	Keeping the Sabbath Holy	34
Day 10	The Twelve Disciples	40
Day 11	The Eternal Sin	44
Day 12	The Parable of the Sower—Part 1	48
Day 13	The Parable of the Sower—Part 2	53
Day 14	The King and his Kingdom	59
Day 15	The Demon-Possessed Man	63
Day 16	The Sick Woman	67
Day 17	The Dead Girl	71
Day 18	Fishing for People	75

Contents

Day 19	Rest and Miracles	79
Day 20	The Heart of a Pharisee	83
Day 21	The Gentile Woman	87
Day 22	The Deaf Man	91
Day 23	Feeding Thousands	95
Day 24	The Way of the Cross	99
Day 25	The Transfiguration	103
Day 26	Greatness in God's Kingdom	107
Day 27	Divorce and Marriage	111
Day 28	The Rich and the Kingdom of God	115
Day 29	Bartimaeus	119
Day 30	King Jesus	123
Day 31	The Noble Vineyard Owner and His Son	127
Day 32	Love the Lord your God	131
Day 33	Love Your Neighbor	135
Day 34	The Widow's Offering	140
Day 35	Be Ready!	144
Day 36	Jesus Anointed at Bethany	148
Day 37	The Last Supper	153
Day 38	Jesus Arrested	156
Day 39	Peter Disowns Jesus	161
Day 40	King of the Jews	165
Day 41	The Death of Jesus	170
Day 42	The Cross of Love	174
Day 43	Some Surprising Disciples	179
Day 44	The Resurrected Christ	184
Day 45	Resurrection Life	189
Bibliography		195

Series Preface

ALL AROUND US PEOPLE are living restless lives, searching everywhere for contentment but never quite finding it. They're always on the move, flitting from one love to another, seeking meaning and purpose. They're constantly changing what they buy, what they look like, what they do, who they're with, where they are. And yet the ache for something more never quite goes away.

If you're tired of the endless searching, and long for a deeply rooted life, the Bible is the exact right place to be.

It's where you'll find joy that fills your heart right up to overflowing.

It's where you'll find hope that never fails.

It's where you'll find an identity that can't be taken away from you.

It's where you'll find the steadfast love your heart aches for.

It's where you'll find rest.

Not because the Bible is all about you. But because the Bible is where we get to know God. The Bible is God's story. It's about who he is and what he's done. And inside the story of God is where we find out who we are, and what life is all about. Inside God's story is where we're given the freedom and safety to finally set down our roots in a firm foundation that will never disappoint us.

The Bible is also the main way God speaks to us, teaching us, encouraging us, challenging us, transforming us, and empowering us. But it can be really hard to know where to start reading the Bible. Even once we do start reading, it can sometimes be confusing and difficult to understand. The Growing Roots series is designed to help you get started reading the Bible for yourself, one book at a time. Studying whole books of the Bible is really important so that we can hear God's full message to us, instead of focusing on just the most famous verses and topics. It shapes our understanding of the whole Bible as one beautiful picture of who our amazing God is.

Developing a daily rhythm of reading through whole books of the Bible will also help your spiritual roots grow deep and strong. Healthy roots don't grow instantly. They develop slowly, day by day, bit by bit. The stronger they grow over time, the more they're able to bring life to the plant above. In Psalm 1, people who enjoy God's word every day are described as being "like a tree planted by streams of water," leafy and fruitful and flourishing. This has been my prayer over you as I write: that as you go deep into the Bible each day, your faith will grow more alive and rich. That your love-relationship with God will blossom beautifully, just like a tree with deep roots that's planted next to a life-giving stream. That through his word, God will nourish and sustain you, deeply refreshing you and satisfying you in a way you never imagined could be possible.

Reading the Bible and praying every day isn't always easy, but the best things in life are never the easiest things. And I promise you: It will be abundantly, overwhelmingly, gloriously worth the effort. Walking closely with God every day is the best thing you'll ever do. Jesus promises that when we seek him we'll find him. And Jesus *always* keeps his promises. So keep making the choice to invest your precious time today and tomorrow and every day after that in the only thing that really matters: knowing God. Pursue him. Run after him as if your life depends on it. Because it does. And you know what? He's already pursuing you, waiting for you with open arms and love in his eyes.

Then you will call upon me and pray to me
And I will listen to you.
You will seek me and find me
When you seek me with all your heart.
(Jeremiah 29:12–13)

Series Preface

How to use this book

What you'll need:

- Some alone time in a quiet place, preferably at the start of each new day.
- Your Bible. In this book I quote the NIV, but you can you use any version.
- This devotional book.
- A journal to write your thoughts and notes in (optional).
- A pen or pencil.

The process:

1. **Prayer**. We should always start our time with God in humble prayer. Ask God to open your heart and mind to be able to understand what you're about to read. Ask that he would show you more of who he is, and who he made you to be. Pray that he would be honored by your desire to get to know him.
2. **Bible**. In your Bible, read the verses indicated at the top of the page in this devotional book. Feel free to read it more than once, and even to write notes in the margins or underline things as you go. I always find that helps me remember the most interesting and important things later on.
3. **Study notes**. Read the notes on the Bible passage in this devotional book. Once again, it can be helpful to write your thoughts in the margins, or underline interesting things as you go.
4. **Reflection questions**. Answer the reflection questions at the end of the devotional notes, using your journal if you want to write your answers down. Take your time to really think them though, and answer honestly. This is not a test; no one will be reading or judging your answers afterwards. They're for you alone, to help you think carefully and deeply about how to apply what you've just read in God's word to your own life.

5. **Prayer.** Talk to God about what you read. You can use the prayer at the end of the reflection questions, or you can pray whatever's in your own heart. Or you can do both!

6. **Meditation.** A Bible verse is provided for you to meditate on throughout the day. Christian meditation means to think carefully about, dwell on, pray through, and reflect on what God has revealed about himself in the Bible. The meditation verse will be short, but it will remind you of one of the key ideas from your devotions. Keep a photo of it on your phone, or write it on your hand or on a small notecard in your wallet, so that you can keep focusing on it as you go through your day.

Introduction to the Gospel of Mark

EVERY BOOK IN THE Bible was written by a human being, but inspired by the Holy Spirit. How this works exactly is one of the amazing mysteries of God, but it means the Bible you have in front of you is 100 percent the words of God and 100 percent the words of the human authors who wrote it. Each book also has its own unique genre (style and structure), and original audience, and it's important that we understand a bit of that context around the book of Mark before we start reading.

Who wrote it:	It was written by John Mark, a Jewish Christian who was the disciple of Simon Peter (one of Jesus' disciples). John Mark wrote down Peter's eye-witness accounts of Jesus' ministry.
When it was written:	It is generally believed to have been written 20–30 years after the end of Jesus' life.
Genre:	This type of text is called Gospel, which is basically a biography. It is a story of the life of Jesus, based on Peter's eye-witness testimony.
Original audience:	This book was written for Christians who didn't have a Jewish background, probably in Rome. They wouldn't have been very familiar with Hebrew words and Jewish traditions, which is why Mark explains some of them in detail.

Day 1

The Good News

(Read Mark 1:1–3)

Simon Peter was one of Jesus' closest disciples, and a leader in the very first Christian churches. John Mark—the author of this book of the Bible—worked for Peter as his scribe, which means his job was to write down Peter's eye-witness testimony of the life of Jesus. Isn't that an incredible thing to think about? The words you've just read in your Bible were first written almost two thousand years ago, capturing the memories from one of the people closest to Jesus in all the world. A real guy who actually walked with Jesus and ate with him and laughed with him! It's quite overwhelming to imagine Mark sitting down at a desk to write and write and write, asking Peter lots of detailed questions, and carefully putting his words down on paper. Imagine as well the pathway those words have taken over the centuries and millennia to finally make their way into your hands today! It all feels a tiny bit miraculous. Thank you God for Peter and for Mark and for the gift of the Bible.

So, where would you expect a book about Jesus to begin? Mark starts this biography in a pretty radical way. Instead of opening with Jesus' family background or birth or childhood, he jumps straight into verse 1 with a huge announcement: Jesus is the *Messiah*! He's the *Son of God*! And he was *prophesied about* many generations before! Let's go deeper into what Mark tells us about Jesus in this verse, and explore why it is such a big deal.

Good news

Some versions of the Bible translate Mark 1:1 as "the gospel of" Jesus. The word 'gospel' simply means 'good news'. It's easy to think of the Bible as a book of advice that tells us the best way to live. But Mark is emphasizing from the very start that the story of Jesus is good *news*, not good *advice*. Advice tells us, "this is how you have to live in order to earn your way to God." But the good news of the Bible says, "This is what has been done in history. This is how Jesus lived and died to earn the way to God for you."[1] See the difference? One is something you have to do to be saved, the other is something that's already been done for you to save you.

The Bible isn't a self-help book. It's not a guide to living your best life. It's not a giant to-do list so you can make it into heaven. It's not actually a book that's mainly about you at all. The Bible exists to tell the good news about who God is and what he's already done for us through Jesus. It's God's way of telling us about himself in a way that we can understand, in written human words that don't change or fade away over the millennia. The Bible is God's story.

Jesus the Messiah

In the first verse, Mark explains that this good news is about Jesus the Messiah. In Hebrew (the Jewish language) *Messiah* means 'the anointed one' or 'the chosen one.' Mark originally wrote his Gospel in Greek, and the Greek translation of this same word is *Christ*. To Jewish people the word Messiah was loaded with a lot of history and hope. In the Old Testament, God promised he would send his people a Messiah to rescue and lead them. Many generations of Jewish people had been longing for the time when this savior would finally come. They hoped he would be a mighty teacher and leader who would free them from the oppression of other kings and empires and bring about a victorious new era for the Jewish people. So for Mark to say that Jesus—a craftsman from the ordinary little village of Nazareth—was actually the Messiah, was a very bold and controversial claim! Jesus was nothing like the powerful warrior king everyone was hoping for.

It's so heart-breaking that some of the people who were desperately longing for the Messiah didn't recognize Jesus when he was standing right in front of them. They missed God's answer to their prayers because he didn't match their expectations. They thought God had promised one

---

1. Keller, *Kings Cross*, 15.

thing, when really he had promised something different but better. Don't judge them—it can be easy for us to make the same tragic mistake. As you read through Mark's Gospel, ask yourself: Is Jesus different from what you expect the God of the universe to be like? Are you disappointed with the way he works, or the people he works through? Do you wish he'd do things in ways that make more sense to you? You aren't alone. Just keep your eyes fixed on Jesus. Pray for God to show you the hidden beauty and glory of Jesus the Messiah. Ask for eyes to see him for who he really is, so that you aren't looking in the wrong direction when he shows up in your own story.

Jesus the Son of God

Have you ever wondered what all of the complicated religious laws and rituals in the Old Testament are about? They're about God's holiness. They teach us that the distance between God and humans is bigger than we could ever imagine. They teach us that we can't just worship God however we like. The Israelites weren't allowed into God's presence except under very specific circumstances. They would die if they looked at his face. By the time of Jesus, Jewish people had even stopped saying the name of God out loud, because they considered it to be too sacred. So at the center of the Old Testament understanding of God is this fact that God is supremely holy. He is infinitely set apart from us. We are completely unworthy to come into His presence.

So, when Mark announces in verse 1 that Jesus is the Son of God, it's *scandalous*. To the Jewish people around Jesus, it would have been incredibly disrespectful to even imagine that this holy God had a child, and that he walked around among normal people. How could this majestic God send his own son down to be born in a fragile human body and grow up in a humble little village? How could this perfect God have a son who needed a bath and pooped and brushed his teeth and had a job just like everyone else?

It *is* pretty crazy when you think about it that way. But the other thing the Old Testament teaches us about God is that he does whatever it takes to make a way for his beloved people to be with him. He is a holy God who chases after unworthy people and invites them into his presence. The only way we can be in a relationship with this kind of God is if *he* makes it possible. God sent us Jesus to bridge the infinite gap between heaven and earth. He sent us his Son to be Immanuel, a name which means 'God with us'. Mark writes it so simply, but saying that Jesus is the Son of God is an earth-shattering, life-changing claim!

As it is written

Mark wraps up his introduction by saying that Jesus had been prophesied about 800 years beforehand by the prophet Isaiah. It's incredible to think about God keeping a promise that he made so many generations before. I'm sure that in the meantime lots of faithful Jewish people had died feeling disappointed, wondering if God had forgotten his promise to them.

Mark encourages us here that God always keeps his promises, in his own perfect time, and in ways we never could have imagined or expected. God can see all of human history in a single glance, and knows what we need most and exactly when we need it. Waiting patiently for God can be one of the hardest things in life. But the more we get to know the character of God and personally experience his love for us, the more we see that he's trustworthy and faithful. We can rest in his promises. He'll never fail us.

Reflect and respond

1. Do you tend to read the Bible as good advice, or as good news?
2. Why are you reading the Gospel of Mark? What do you hope to get out of it?
3. Meditate for a few moments on the idea of Jesus as Immanuel, 'God with us.' How does it lead you to worship God more today?

The Good News

Lord God,
I am in awe of your perfect holiness.
I'll never be able to fully understand just how good and righteous and pure you are.
Help me see you more clearly as I study the life of Jesus in the book of Mark.
I want to really know you, and really experience you.
I want to taste and see that you're good, and trustworthy, and faithful.
I want to rest in you, believing that you know what's best for me.
I want to trust in your promises.

In Jesus name,
Amen

Meditation verse for the day:

The beginning of the good news
about Jesus the Messiah, the Son of God.
(Mark 1:1)

Day 2

Jesus' Baptism

(Read Mark 1:4–11)

There are four gospels in the Bible: Matthew, Mark, Luke, and John. They were all written by different people, at different times, in different styles, to different audiences, about the same topic: Jesus. Each Gospel focuses on different parts of Jesus' life and his teaching based on different eye-witness testimonies, so not every detail is included in every Gospel. However, the story of Jesus' baptism is included in all four Gospels, so clearly this is a very important event that all his biographers wanted us to know about.

John the Baptist

John the Baptist was quirky. He was an outsider. And yet God chose him to be the last of Israel's great prophets. This is how God acts all the way through the Bible: He *never* chooses the people our culture says are the best. He doesn't do his mightiest works through the smartest, richest, or most attractive people. God consistently uses the least likely people for the most important jobs. Even Jesus himself grew up in the small town of Nazareth, which was considered a backward little country village where nothing good ever happened.

The best thing about John the Baptist isn't his weird clothing or the strange food he ate. All four Gospels tell us that even though he had huge crowds of people following him, he was an incredibly humble guy. He told anyone who would listen that he wasn't even worthy to untie Jesus' sandals. He was overjoyed when the crowds left him and started following Jesus instead, explaining, "He must become greater; I must become less" (John 3:30). This is what humility actually is: having the right perspective on who we are in relation to who God is. Humble people point all the honor they get in life back to God. Humble people know that everything they have and everything they achieve is actually a gift from God. And our good God just loves to show his power through weak people who fully depend on him. He invites humble people like John to play beautiful parts in his salvation story!

The Trinity

When Jesus is baptized, something incredible happens. We see God, Jesus, and the Holy Spirit united and celebrating together (verses 10 and 11). The Holy Spirit gently pours down his presence from heaven. God publicly tells Jesus how much he adores him. This loving three-way relationship is what we call the Trinity. 'Trinity' isn't a word you'll find in the Bible, but it describes the way that God is *one* God in *three* beings. He is God the Father, and he is also God the Son, and he is also God the Spirit, all at the same time. All of them are one and the same, but they are also all unique and separate. They have different roles, but they're all equal and they love to honor and glorify one another in everything they do. They've existed forever together in perfect unity and joy, and we get a tiny peek into that incredible relationship at Jesus' baptism.

The Trinity is one of those things about God that's impossible for our human brains to really comprehend. We literally don't have the language to explain how it's possible, because God exists on a whole other level from us. So get comfortable with the idea that you'll never fully understand God, and let that mystery lead you to worship him. He's magnificent! He's breathtaking! He deserves all our awe and reverence! He's so far beyond us that we can't even get our heads around how he exists in the way he does. And yet the amazing thing is that God invites us to enter into his intimate Trinity-love. He's saying to you today, "I am Love. Will you let me love you?"

God's love for Jesus

Read God's words to his beloved Son again in verse 11. If we're honest, lots of us long to hear words like that from our own fathers. Too many people have fathers who only use their words to criticize or tear down. Some people have tragically never even heard the sound of their father's voice.

In this passage, we see the beautiful way that God loves Jesus. He affirms their intimate relationship: "You are my Son." He affirms how he feels about Jesus: "I love you, and I am so pleased with you." Keep in mind that this takes place at the very *start* of Jesus' public ministry. He hasn't done miracles yet. He hasn't preached to huge crowds yet. He isn't famous yet. He hasn't brought anyone back to life yet. He hasn't achieved the mission he was sent to earth for yet. He's just a normal thirty-year old guy from a small town. And still God is pleased by him. Not just a bit pleased, but well pleased. Very pleased. Jesus makes God *so* happy.

Maybe you come from a family that really values being a high achiever. Maybe you've been taught that your worth comes from how good you are, how much you do, how hard you work, or how well you perform. Maybe you worry that your family or friends won't love you as much if you fail a test, or lose a championship game, or bomb a performance. Maybe you find it really hard to slow down and rest because it makes you anxious to stop being productive. But when you become a Christian, you become part of God's family. As his adopted child, he speaks the exact same words over you that he spoke over Jesus.

God reassures you, "You are my child."

He smiles at you, "I adore you."

He promises you, "I am so pleased with you."

The Bible tells us that God sings over us with joy, and that he delights in us. He isn't waiting until you've proved yourself. His love isn't dependant on how much you achieve, or how hard you work. He loves you because you're his. No matter what the world thinks of you, your heavenly Father's heart brims with joy when he looks at you, his beloved child. He's smiling over you right now!

Reflect and respond

1. *How does it make you feel to know that God loves to invite unlikely people to be part of his story? Why do you feel that way?*
2. *Meditate on God's feelings towards you as his beloved child. How does it lead you to praise him? How does it lead you to trust him?*

Jesus' Baptism

Father,
Thank you for the Trinity, even though it's too much for me to properly understand.
Thank you that love is at the very center of who you are.
Thank you that you invite me into that love, to be your beloved child.
Help me to trust that no matter who I am or what I've done, I'm yours.
Help me to believe that you delight in me.
Please take away my fear and doubt and give me overwhelming comfort and security in your steadfast love for me.

In Jesus name,
Amen

Meditation verse for the day:

You are my Son, whom I love;
with you I am well pleased.
(Mark 1:11)

Day 3

In the Wilderness

(Read Mark 1:12-13)

Blessings in the wilderness

Mark is famous for writing in a style that includes very few detailed descriptions. But Mark's short explanation of Jesus' time in the wilderness tells us a lot in just three small details. First, Jesus was tempted by Satan. Second, he was with wild animals. And lastly, angels looked after him. Through these three details, Mark is emphasizing that the wilderness wasn't a nice place for Jesus. He wasn't spending these forty days in some kind of self-care retreat away from the busyness of normal life. The wilderness was harsh and uncomfortable. Jesus was in danger both spiritually and physically. But the wilderness was also the place where God provided for Jesus in a unique and special way. Jesus was never alone out there. God sent his angels to minister to him! That is amazingly encouraging.

But how did Jesus end up in this awful place? Verse 12 tells us: "The Spirit sent him out into the wilderness." Is that surprising to you? Why would God's Spirit deliberately send his beloved Jesus somewhere hard and dangerous? (It's worth mentioning here that often we end up in the wilderness because of our own sinful choices or mistakes, or the sin of other people.) But just like he did with Jesus, God does sometimes lead us into dark, difficult places where we're surrounded by things that can really hurt us. Your wilderness might be a season of loneliness, or a move to a new place, or a terrible grief, or financial insecurity. You might feel lost. Your heart might be broken. You may wonder if God really knows what he's doing. It can feel overwhelming not knowing if your wilderness will last for forty days or forty years. In those times, it's really easy to question whether we are where God wants us to be, because hard situations like these don't feel like his best plan for our lives.

But there's actually a pattern throughout the Bible of God deliberately leading his people out into the wilderness, to bless them there and teach them something precious and new about himself. In the emptiness of the desert is where we consistently see God providing wonderfully for his people. He let the Israelites feel desperate hunger and thirst, and then he miraculously provided food and water for them. He let Jesus be tempted by Satan and surrounded by wild animals, but he also sent angels to care for him. Talking about Israel using the metaphor of a cheating wife, God once said, "But then I will win her back once again. I will lead her into the desert and speak tenderly to her there. I will return her vineyards to her and transform the Valley of Trouble into a gateway of hope" (Hosea 2:14–15, NLT). Through these wonderful words we see that God sometimes leads his people into the wilderness as an act of tender, passionate love. In the quiet of the wilderness is where we can finally be still enough to hear his gentle voice singing sweet love songs over us. He takes us to the desert so that he can give us the unexpected gift of fruitfulness and abundant life there. He transforms the pathway through trouble into a doorway to something new and beautiful and full of hope. As painful as it feels, time in the wilderness can be one of the greatest gifts God gives us. Because it's often in the empty, lonely, dangerous places of life that we learn to rely on God more, and then we experience more of his presence and his loving care than ever before.

Responding in the wilderness

Our responsibility once we're in the wilderness is to decide how we're going to respond to being there. Are we going to resent God? Lose faith in his goodness? Doubt his wisdom? Wallow in our loneliness? Focus on everything we've lost? Or are we going to turn our eyes to God and open up our hearts to what he wants to teach us? How we respond to being in the wilderness makes all the difference to our perspective. It still won't be easy and fun and safe. And it won't necessarily mean we'll get out of the wilderness any sooner. But it will completely transform our experience of our suffering, and our relationship with God. The parallel version of this event in Matthew's Gospel tells us how Jesus responded to being in the wilderness: He fasted for the full forty days and forty nights. Fasting in Judasim and Christianity means not eating food for a short period of time in order to draw closer to God spiritually. It means to stop eating temporarily as a symbolic way of saying to God, "I need you more than I need food. Food isn't what's keeping me alive, you are! Sustain me Lord!" So Jesus responds to the wilderness by focusing his whole mind, body, and soul on God. And the result? He was weak physically, but he was spiritually strengthened so that he could resist the devil's temptations.

Psalm 63 also gives us a wonderful example of how we should respond when we find ourselves in the wilderness. King David wrote this psalm while he was escaping through the wilderness from his own son Absalom, who was hunting him down with an army. The heart-breaking story starts in 2 Samuel 15. David had to flee from his home, knowing that if he stayed he would be killed. He was exhausted, hungry, thirsty, and weeping with grief as he ran. His heart was shattered. He'd lost his son, friends, his throne, and was close to losing his life. Everything was going very wrong. And this is the context of Psalm 63.

David starts the psalm crying out to God with all his heart. He doesn't sugar-coat his desperation. He prays to God with complete honesty. He's not trying to be positive. He acknowledges his pain, and begs God to meet him right where he's at. He knows that what he needs most at that moment is more of God. That's why he says in verse 2, "So I have looked upon you in the sanctuary, beholding your power and glory" (ESV). Even though he's suffering, his response isn't to dwell on how awful his situation is. Instead he chooses to focus all his attention on how powerful and glorious his God is. He turns his eyes to God, knowing that he has nothing else left. We see that in verse 6 as well, when David deliberately uses the long, sleepless nights to meditate on God instead of letting his anxious mind run wild with worry. We all know how easy it is to lie in bed for hours, replaying awful conversations and scenarios in our minds or stressing about things that might happen in the future. In my own sleepless nights in the wilderness, I've prayed this psalm hundreds of times. It reminds me not to dwell on my circumstances, guards my heart against self-pity, and helps me keep my mind focused on God.

The beauty of Psalm 63 is that we see God's comfort piercing through the darkness of the wilderness. God graciously shows David that his steadfast love is the most precious thing in all of life. He reminds David that even though he's lost everything else, God's love will never leave him. That's why David can sing in spite of his circumstances. That's why he can have joy and deep contentment in the middle of his mourning. As David cried out in the wilderness, God answered him with an abundance of exactly what David needed most: God himself.

So if you're in a wilderness season of life right now, don't give up hope. Lean into God with all you have. Cling to him, and see that he really is as good as he says he is. Ask to hear his gentle whisper wooing your heart. Trust him to be everything you need. Beg to experience his steadfast love in a way that satisfies your deepest longings and heals your broken heart. Keep your Bible open and search for glimpses of God's power and glory. Fast and pray. Fix your eyes on who God is. Behold him. Gaze upon him. Pray for your wilderness to become the place where God reveals himself to you in a refreshing and life-changing way.

Reflect and respond

1. *How does it encourage you to know that God deliberately led his beloved Son into a hard, dangerous, lonely place? How can it help you trust him when you're in the wilderness yourself?*
2. *Next time you're in the wilderness, how can you practice depending on God to be all you need?*

Turn to Psalm 63 in your Bible. Pray this psalm out to God today.

Meditation verse for the day:

But then I will win her back once again.
I will lead her into the desert and speak tenderly to her there.
I will return her vineyards to her
and transform the Valley of Trouble into a gateway of hope.
(Hosea 2:14–15, NLT)

Day 4

The Kingdom of God

(Read Mark 1:14–20)

The kingdom of God

In today's verses we finally hear Jesus' speak, and the first thing he says is, "The time has come, the kingdom of God has come near." Jesus is letting God's people know that the Messiah they've been longing for has finally arrived. The wait is over! The time is now! But what exactly is the kingdom of God? This is a really important question, because the kingdom of God is actually the topic Jesus talks about more than anything else. We'll learn a lot more about the kingdom of God as we go through the book of Mark, but here are the basics:

- *What is it?* The kingdom of God (sometimes also called the kingdom of heaven) means God's reign as King. It is not a particular place, like a kingdom on a map with boundaries and borders. It's God's lordship over his people, wherever or whenever they are in history.
- *Why does it exist?* The purpose of the kingdom of God is salvation. Through Jesus, God is at work to save and renew every part of our lives and our world. He rescues us, then transforms us from the inside out. He takes his place as the rightful King of our hearts and lives, restoring us be to the people and community he created us to be in the very beginning.

- *When is this kingdom coming?* God's kingdom comes in two stages: It has already come in part, and one day will come in full. Jesus makes it clear that he's brought the kingdom of God to us. It's here now! However, he also talks about it as something that's not yet completed. It's here, but it's not here *fully* yet. This explains why there is still brokenness and pain in the world. God is patiently giving people a chance to accept or reject his lordship. But one day Jesus will return as the King of kings and Lord of lords to judge the whole earth. Then the kingdom of God will have fully come, with Jesus sitting on the throne for all eternity.

Repentance

The next words out of Jesus' mouth in verse 15 are a command: "Repent and believe the good news!" Repentance means to admit our sin and turn away from it. It doesn't mean we spend our time obsessing over how much we've messed up, focusing on our guilt and feeling terrible about ourselves. We definitely need to see that we're deeply spiritually sick, but only so that it pushes us to ask the doctor for help. God is the doctor we need. Repentance means that we can see how wonderful God truly is, and how desperately we need him, and we're turning away from our sin and towards him as our Lord and Savior. That's why it's important that repenting and believing are two halves of the same action: Repenting is what we're turning away from, and believing shows what we're turning to instead.

Following him

First, Jesus announces the kingdom of God and commands us to repent and believe. Next we hear an invitation: "Come, follow me" (verse 17). For these very first disciples, he means to literally follow him. Walk with him. Do life together with him. Jesus was a rabbi, which means 'teacher'. Rabbis were Jewish spiritual leaders and religious teachers whose disciples followed them everywhere, listening to them and trying to be like them. Disciples were students, like apprentices learning from their master.

Pastor Eugene Peterson wrote a book called *The Jesus Way* about what it means for us to follow Jesus as his disciples today. He says, "To follow Jesus means that we can't separate what Jesus is saying from what Jesus is doing and the way that He is doing it."[1] Peterson explains that being a disciple of Jesus isn't *just* believing the stuff Jesus says. It means we also carefully watch how Jesus speaks and thinks and acts and prays and treats others, and over time as we walk beside him through life we learn how to speak and think and act and pray and treat others that same way.

Maybe you've been told that you need to choose your friends wisely, because who you hang out with is probably who you'll become like. The people we do life with influence us and change us, bit by bit over time. The more time we spend with them, the more we start to speak like them, and think like them, and act like them. They rub off on us. It's the same thing with being a follower of Jesus. He wants you to spend quality time with him every day because you love him. He wants you to meditate on the words he speaks until they're written on your heart. He wants you to follow in his footsteps, living out what he teaches you everywhere you go. The best part is that he invites you to follow him because he loves you and he knows it's the best thing for you. He is the Way, the Truth and the Life. He wants you to follow his way, to find real truth and discover the best kind of life. And the Bible promises that when we consistently spend quality time with Jesus, the Holy Spirit gradually transforms our hearts and lives into more and more glorious, holy, beautiful reflections of him. When we follow Jesus, we become like Jesus! What an incredible promise!

One of the best parts of all this is how simple the process is. Jesus doesn't say, "Come follow me, once you've stopped sinning so much." He doesn't say, "Come follow me after you deal with your anxiety and depression." He doesn't say, "Come follow me, once you pass this Bible knowledge quiz." He only says two simple things:

- *"Come, follow me"*: He invites us just as we are, right this very moment, to walk with him and be close to him and be one of his people.
- *"I will send you out to fish for people"*: When we decide to follow him, he gives us a whole new purpose in life, and he makes something new and wonderful out of us.

There's absolutely nothing we have to do to qualify to be a disciple of Jesus: He welcomes us exactly as we are. We don't have to be smart, or popular, or confident, or mentally healthy. We don't have to have our lives in order. *All we have to do is receive his invitation.* I love that all through the Gospels we see sick, broken people crossing paths with Jesus and leaving

---

1. Peterson, *The Jesus Way*, 22.

his presence changed. You see, Jesus calls us just as we are, but he never leaves us that way. He transforms us. He teaches us. He helps us grow. He brings us healing, hope, comfort, and joy. He gives our hearts a new song to sing! And he sends us out into the world to "fish for people," which means carrying his loving invitation to the people around us, so that more and more of us can sing for joy together!

Reflect and respond

1. *What's an area of your life that you struggle to let Jesus be king in? What do you find it hard to trust him with, or to obey him in? If you find this question difficult to answer, spend some time praying that God would show you.*
2. *What do you love most about Jesus? What makes you want to follow him and be near him and become like him?*

Loving Father,
I can never thank you enough for the invitation you offer me through Jesus.
I want to follow him.
I'm sorry that I usually give my time and energy to being a disciple to other people instead.
Give me a passion for following Jesus alone.
Holy Spirit, help me understand what I read in the Bible, so that I can learn and grow.
Set my heart on fire for Jesus, so that he is my first love.
Please transform me from the inside out so that everyone around me can see I'm becoming more and more like my rabbi, Jesus.

In Jesus name,
Amen

Meditation verse for the day:

"Come, follow me," Jesus said,
"and I will send you out to fish for people."
(Mark 1:17)

Day 5

The Authority of Jesus

(READ MARK 1:21-39)

Teaching and healing with authority

MARK DOESN'T TELL US many details about Jesus' first time teaching in the synagogue. (A synagogue is a Jewish place of worship, like a church.) But his main point is very clear: Jesus dramatically demonstrates his authority for all to see. Nobody can deny it. In verse 22 we see that everyone who hears his preaching is astonished. They must have seen that he didn't just know a lot *about* God, but he actually knew God intimately and personally. He must have spoken boldly and passionately, rooted in the deep assurance and confidence that comes from knowing exactly who his Father is. Have you ever met someone who talks about God like this?

Then suddenly a demon-possessed man starts loudly disrupting the service. The demon recognizes who Jesus really is, and in verse 24 he calls him both his human name—"Jesus of Nazareth"—and his Old Testament Messiah name—"The Holy One of God!" Jesus responds sternly but calmly, speaking just a few simple words. There's no fiery battle or big spiritual showdown. The demon has no choice but to obey Jesus, and the man is instantly set free.

In verses 21-34, Mark continues to show us that Jesus is a man with absolute authority. He speaks about God with authority. He has authority over evil spirits. He heals sick people with just a touch. He is sovereign (in total control) over everything in creation! We sometimes get so used to the stories of Jesus healing people that we just skim quickly over these paragraphs, but can you imagine being there and watching him do these incredible things? Can you imagine disabled bodies being healed on the spot? Soul-sucking mental illnesses being immediately lifted? People must have been shouting and crying with shock and joy! It would have been the greatest day of some of these people's entire lives! Don't skim over these stories: they are so important. Jesus supernaturally powerful actions in this passage are saying to us, "Listen to me. Believe me. I deserve your trust. I deserve your worship. I deserve your obedience. I deserve to have ultimate authority in your life, because of who I AM. I am Lord over all creation, and I am your rightful King."

Who has authority in your life?

Now think about your own relationship with Jesus. Does he have the ultimate authority in your life? In other words, do you happily submit to his right to rule over you? Have you surrendered all that you are to him? Do you trust his wisdom in deciding what should happen to you and how it should happen? Do you obey what he tells you to do without questioning his goodness? Does he reign over your thoughts and emotions and conversations and actions?

Our world says that the most important thing in life is to do what feels good to us. We're told that if our hearts say something is true for us, then it is. We're taught that if it feels natural to us then it must be right for us. We're encouraged to follow our desires and define our own truth. We don't like the idea of having a king, even if he is a kind and good one. We don't want someone else to tell us what to do; we want to be in control. We believe that we know what's best for us. We want to sit on the throne in our own lives. But the Bible teaches us that this is the path to destruction and pain.

In today's passage, Mark shows us that Jesus has unquestionable authority over all of creation. Jesus has every right to be your Lord and Master and King, but he won't ever force you to respect and obey him. He wants you to willingly choose to follow him, trusting that wherever he leads you will be the best thing for you. He wants you to delight in submitting to him, knowing that he is righteous and holy and good.

Jesus prays in a solitary place

Even though Jesus was up late healing the huge crowds of people who were gathered around his door, verse 35 tells us that he got up before sunrise the next day to pray. We don't know how long he was praying for, but we do know it was long enough that everyone else started looking for him. Clearly, quality time with God is his number one priority, more important to him than sleep or healing more people or preaching to the crowds. He genuinely loves being with God and doesn't want anything or anyone else to get in the way. He considers his time alone with his Father to be absolutely non-negotiable. Remember back at the start of today's passage, where we read that people were amazed at Jesus' preaching? *This* is where his authority came from. This is how he got to know God so well that he could speak with such power and confidence. Rich, regular, intimate time with God. Jesus wasn't just reading words off a dusty old scroll, he was talking about the real person he was closest to in the whole world!

Reflect on the time you spend alone with God. How regularly do you get away from all the busyness of life, put your phone away, and prioritize simply being with him in a quiet place? What does prayer-time look like for you? Let's be totally honest: a lot of the time, prayer isn't really something we think of as productive time. Sometimes it can feel boring, or it's hard to keep our minds focused on God for more than a few minutes. Often when we pray, we treat God like a sort of fairy godfather, listing off all the things we need him to do for us.

But God's not Santa, he's your adoring Father. Being a child of God is a relationship of love. And healthy relationships can't last without lots of communication. No deep love will flourish without regular, honest talking and listening. We talk to our close friends so much because we enjoy sharing life with them! Prayer is the same. God already knows what's happening in your life, but he still wants to hear it from you. He wants you to run to him all throughout the day with your thoughts and feelings, because you enjoy talking with him and listening to him. He's honored when we prioritize him by making time to be with him away from the noise of daily life. He invites us to get intimate with him through prayer, talking to him and leaving space to listen to him. He wants us to pray because we're passionate about knowing him more, not because we're passionate about getting things from him. So set aside quality time every day to be fully present to him, and I promise it will change your whole life.

The Authority of Jesus

Reflect and respond

1. *Who or what has the ultimate authority in your life? It might be another person, a belief system, or yourself.*
2. *Reflect on the authority of Jesus over all of the created world. How does it encourage you to trust him with your whole life?*
3. *How does today's reading challenge you to pray differently? What might this look like on a daily basis?*

Lord of all creation,
All power and authority on heaven and earth are yours.
I worship you in awe of who you are!
Who am I, that you love me?
Who am I, that you invite me to pray to you anytime, about anything?
Thank you for being my loving Father and my sovereign Master.
Please help me to joyfully submit to you as my King.
Please help me to delight in your authority and trust in your wisdom.
Please teach me to cherish the gift of prayer.

In Jesus name,
Amen

Meditation verse for the day:

For in [Jesus] all things were created:
things in heaven and on earth, visible and invisible ...
all things have been created through him and for him.
(Colossians 1:16)

Day 6

The Man with Leprosy

(Read Mark 1:40–45)

In ancient times, leprosy was a name given to a range of different skin conditions, and it was a life-changing diagnosis. People with leprosy were social outcasts. No one would go near them, because people were afraid of catching their disease. They weren't allowed to worship God in the synagogue because they were considered to be ceremonially unclean. Their disease was visible on their skin to anyone who saw them, and they were judged and rejected every day of their lonely, painful lives.

Jesus touches a man with leprosy

Mark's Gospel is famous for being written in simple, undramatic language, so don't miss how radical this moment is. When verse 41 tells us that Jesus "reached out his hand and touched the man," this is *big*. It is not socially acceptable behavior! The people around Jesus probably gasped out loud in disgust, wondering if he'd gone mad. Nobody touched people with leprosy. Nobody except Jesus.

We know from plenty of other examples in the Gospels that Jesus didn't need to physically touch someone to heal them. Jesus could easily have healed this man with just a word or a thought. But Jesus deliberately reaches out and touches someone who no one else would even dream of touching. This man might not have been touched in years, or decades! Can you even begin to imagine how he would have felt? Scientists have found that physical touch is crucial for all human flourishing. Newborn babies need lots of touch to grow healthy brains and emotional connections. Adults who are deprived of human touch are much more likely to be depressed, anxious, stressed, and to get sick more often. Healthy human touch also connects us powerfully to other people in emotional and relational ways. That's why pastor Rich Villodas says that "in demonstrating the power of God through human touch, Jesus was not just healing a body; he was restoring community."[1] He's welcoming him back into the community that has kept him at a distance for so long, back to family and friends and neighbors and hugs and kisses. Jesus is touching this unclean man and giving him his own cleanness. Which—spiritually speaking—is exactly what Jesus does with every one of us.

Jesus is love

Verse 41 tells us in various translations that Jesus was "moved with compassion," "moved with pity and sympathy," or "deeply moved." Jesus doesn't heal this man just to prove he has authority over diseases; he heals him because he's filled with empathy and care for him. His heart is moved by the hopelessness and loneliness he sees in this isolated man, and in overflowing compassion he reaches out and gently touches him, and heals him.

In his beautiful book about Jesus called *Gentle and Lowly*, pastor Dane Ortlund writes, "The Jesus given to us in the Gospels is not simply one who loves, but one who is love; merciful affections stream from his innermost heart as rays from the sun."[2] Read that again and let it sink deep into your heart. Jesus doesn't just act lovingly towards us, he actually *is* love in human form. Every single thing about his character and nature and being is the deepest and truest form of love we could ever imagine. He is literally the walking definition of Love, complete and whole and perfect.

And Ortlund says, "merciful affections stream from his innermost heart." This means that Jesus doesn't just love us, he also likes us! He feels deep, warm affection for us. Not because we're particularly likeable or worthy, but simply because of how incredibly loving he is. The Bible tells us that God delights in his people (Psalm 147:11), that he rejoices with all his heart and soul in doing good for us (Jeremiah 32:41), and that he lovingly sings songs of gladness over us (Zephaniah 3:17). He isn't just putting up with us

1. Villodas, *Deeply Formed Life*, 163.
2. Ortlund, *Gentle and Lowly*, 27.

because he feels sorry for us. He enjoys us, and wants an intimate relationship with us, and longs to bring us true healing and freedom and joy!

Picture the crowds standing around this poor man with leprosy. All of them would have been hanging back. Some of them might have been holding their clothes up over their noses and mouths, others might have their noses crinkled, or disgust and fear on their faces. But Jesus doesn't. He doesn't hold his nose or cringe inside or take a step back so that he can heal this man from a comfortable distance. He doesn't judge the guy based on his appearance, or look down on him. Jesus lovingly comes close to the suffering man. He deliberately steps nearer when everyone else steps away. He reaches out his hand and touches him, gently letting him know that he's not alone.

Jesus loves you

Chances are you don't have leprosy. But you can probably relate to this man in some way—all of us can. Maybe your shame is secretly hidden away deep inside you, or maybe it's public and visible for all to see. You might feel judged and rejected by the people around you. You might feel lonely, like an outsider who doesn't quite belong anywhere. You might long for healing that seems impossible. You might just want to feel seen and loved.

This story is for you today.

Let this Jesus who is Love walk up to you right where you are. Let him get close. See the compassion in his eyes, and hear the gentleness in his voice. Show him the deep pain that you keep hidden from the rest of the world. You're safe in his caring hands. Feel the warmth and tenderness in his touch. He knows every single thing about you, and he isn't disgusted by you. He isn't disappointed in you. He loves you and delights in you. He's passionate about bringing healing to all the hurt places in your life. He longs to make you whole. You can trust him. You can trust his love for you.

Reflect and respond

1. *What has God shown you about himself through this passage?*
2. *In what ways are you like the man with leprosy?*
3. *Meditate on the fact that God loves you, and that thinking about you makes him sing with joy. How does it change how you think about him?*

The Man with Leprosy

God of love,
In Isaiah 49 you tell me that before I was born you called my name.
You tell me that I'm honored in your eyes.
You promise to guide me in a way that's good for me.
You say that you'll comfort me and have compassion on me when I'm going through hard things.
You remind me that my name is eternally engraved on the palms of your hands, so you'll never forget me.
Thank you that you love me so deeply and so well!
I love you.

In Jesus name,
Amen

Meditation verse for the day:

For the Lord your God is living among you.
He is a mighty savior.
He will take delight in you with gladness.
With his love, he will calm all your fears.
He will rejoice over you with joyful songs.
(Zephaniah 3:17, NLT)

Day 7

The Paralyzed Man

(READ MARK 2:1–12)

The spiritual authority of Jesus

LIKE SO MUCH OF Mark's story so far, this passage teaches us about both the authority of Jesus and the love of Jesus. Jesus forgives this man's sins, demonstrating his absolute spiritual authority. The teachers of the law are immediately scandalized, because they know that only God has the authority to forgive sins. They realize that Jesus is pretty much saying, "I am God!" and they're not happy about it. This anger will eventually lead to their plan to kill him.

If you've repented for your sins and asked Jesus for his forgiveness, his words in verse 5 are also for you: "Child, your sins are forgiven." This means that Jesus has paid the price for all of your sins—past, present and future. God looks at your record and sees only the perfection of Jesus, and welcomes you gladly into his presence for all eternity. We should never stop feeling amazement and awe at this all the days of our lives!

If we're honest though, we sometimes live as if Jesus doesn't actually have the authority to forgive our sins. We think and act like we're still enslaved to sin, as if the King of kings never broke the power sin had over us. We feel like our sin will always rule us, and that we have no hope of ever defeating it. Does that describe you? If you're struggling to believe that Jesus really has authority to forgive your sins, stop and pray about it right now. Faith is a gift from God—*ask him for it*! Ask him to help you trust him more. Ask him to help your beliefs line up with the truth of God and not the lies of the devil. Ask him to powerfully show you that he has already set you free from being a slave to sin. Ask the Holy Spirit to bring you the freedom of a child of God!

The love of Jesus

Next, Jesus heals the man's body, showing his authority over creation. Not even the world's greatest doctors can heal a sick person by simply speaking a few words! But Jesus has complete power to heal the human body, anytime he chooses to. Through this healing, we're also shown the lovingkindness of Jesus. Firstly, in the obvious way: his language. He looks at this man and clearly feels a deep empathy for him, tenderly calling him "son." But the love of Jesus is displayed in a much more subtle way here as well. Have you ever wondered why Jesus forgave the man's sins first, instead of healing his body straight away?

Think about it: By now Jesus is famous for healing people. This man's courageous friends are so desperate to get him in front of Jesus that they literally break through the roof to find a way in. I'm sure there was an awkward silence in the room after Jesus spoke the words, "Son, your sins are forgiven." His friends were probably thinking, "Ahh, thanks a lot but you've misunderstood what we're here for. We were actually hoping you'd heal his paralysis. . ."

So why did Jesus do this and what does it have to do with his love? Pastor Timothy Keller explains: "Jesus knows something the man doesn't know—that he has a much bigger problem than his physical condition. Jesus is saying to him, "I understand your problems. I have seen your suffering. I'm going to get to that. But please realize that the main problem in a person's life is never his suffering; it's his sin.""[1]

Jesus looks at this man and loves him. He loves him so much that he doesn't want to just give him what he *wants* most, but what he *needs* most. You see, physical healing is wonderful, but it only lasts for this lifetime. Our bodies will all eventually die of something. But when our sins are forgiven and we are adopted by God, that changes our whole eternity. It sets us on a path to discovering the meaning of our existence, and the deepest joys known to human beings both in this life and forever. Forgiveness is the

---

1. Keller, *King's Cross*, 27–28.

greatest gift Jesus can ever give, and he gives it to this man immediately and freely, even though he hadn't asked for it. This man left Jesus' presence that day changed forever. He had received more than he could have ever imagined, and exactly what he needed most in all the world.

It's not wrong to pray for the things you want and think you need. God cares about all the details of our lives and delights in giving his children good gifts. He wants us to bring all our burdens to him in prayer. But always remember that God knows you better than you know yourself, and he wants to lavish on you much more than you will ever dream of asking for. It might look very different than you imagined. He might say "No" to what you think you need so that he can give you an infinitely better "Yes." Or he might ask you to trust him while he uses your suffering to bring you to a place where you're ready for deeper spiritual healing. This can be really hard. But God promises to be your kind, wise Father. Do you believe that he loves you enough to give you what you ultimately need most, instead of just what you want in the moment?

Choose godly friends

This beautiful story also reminds us how important it is to have close friends who love God. This man can't walk himself to Jesus. But he has friends who are willing to do whatever it takes to get him into Jesus' presence, and it changes his life forever. All good friends are a wonderful gift. They can be encouraging and helpful and loving and fun and kind. But only solid Christian friends will do whatever it takes to bring us to the feet of Jesus in our hardest times. They know that what we need most in our suffering is God, and they'll do anything to help us draw close to him. When we don't have the strength to pray, they will stand in the gap and pray for us. When we can't see past our pain, they help us fix our eyes on Jesus. When all we can hear are the lies of the Enemy, they lovingly remind us of the kind, gentle voice of our Father. When we're sinking in our shame, they remind us that God has already forgiven us and is welcoming us back with open arms. And when we can't even drag ourselves into God's presence, they break open the roof and carry us there. Do you have Christian friends like that? Are you that kind of friend to others?

Reflect and respond

1. Reflect on the idea that the biggest problem in your life is your own sinfulness. How does that challenge you to think and pray differently about your sin?
2. What is something beautiful about God that you've seen through this passage?
3. Do you have at least one Christian friend who carries you into Jesus' presence when you need it most? If not, how can you start developing a friendship like that? Who can you be that kind of friend to?

In your Bible, turn to 1 Chronicles 29:10–13. Pray King David's prayer of praise to God, worshiping him for his incomparable authority and love.

Meditation verse for the day:

When Jesus saw their faith,
he said to the paralyzed man,
"Son, your sins are forgiven."
(Mark 2:5)

Day 8

Jesus Welcomes Sinners

(Read Mark 2:13–17)

In today's passage Jesus calls another disciple to follow him: Levi the tax collector. Like lots of people back then, Levi had two names. He was called Levi in Hebrew and Matthew in Greek. This is actually the same man who eventually wrote the Gospel of Matthew, the first book in the New Testament.

Jesus welcomes a tax collector

In Jesus' time, this part of the world belonged to the Roman Empire. This means that Rome had conquered the Jewish lands and now ruled over them with their own soldiers and laws. A tax collector like Levi worked for the Roman Empire, collecting taxes from the Jewish people and sending the money off to Rome. They were also well-known for lying about how much tax people owed, then keeping the extra money for themselves instead of handing it all over to Rome. It's not surprising that many Jewish people hated tax collectors and felt like they had betrayed their own people, taking sides with the enemy. Working for Rome made tax collectors powerful, and stealing from their own people made them rich, but it came at the cost of being rejected by their whole community.

For Jesus to invite a hated tax collector to be his disciple would have been almost as scandalous as when he touched a man with leprosy. The people around Jesus must have been very confused. The other disciples were probably pretty angry about it too—no one would have wanted a tax collector to be part of their group!

God's transforming grace

We don't know many details of Levi's life, but we can see where he started and where he ended up. The day Jesus first invited Levi to follow him, Levi jumped at the chance to leave his old life behind. He must have been unhappy with the way he was living, and was desperate for a change. He eagerly left his fancy house and good job behind to join Jesus in traveling all over the countryside, living without a permanent address or the nice food and comfortable bed and luxurious clothes he was used to.

Levi spent the next three years with Jesus as one of his closest friends and disciples, hearing him teach and watching how he lived and following him one step at a time. He never changed his mind and went back to being a tax collector, so we can safely assume that life with Jesus was far better than anything he'd left behind, even without all the power and money. Eventually this same man became one of the most important authors in all of history: the writer of the Gospel of Matthew. God completely changed him from the inside out, and used him to spread the good news throughout the whole world, even thousands of years after his death. Now that's an amazing honor for a man who used to be hated by everyone!

Jesus is inviting you to follow him, just like he did to Levi that day. He's ready to renew and redeem every part of your life. He promises to make you a brand new creation. He wants to use your life to display the glory of his splendor, so that you leave ripples through eternity, just like Levi did. Have you responded to his invitation yet? What are you waiting for?

Healthy vs. sick

After calling Levi to be his disciple, Jesus went over to his house for dinner. Luke's description of this same event in Luke 5 shows us that this is not just any ordinary meal: Levi is throwing a huge feast for Jesus, and has invited a huge crowd of other tax collectors and 'sinners' along. I just love how over and over in the Gospels we see Jesus slowing down and making time in his day for ordinary people. He sits with them, and eats with them, and talks to them. He shares life with them. And these are people that no one else wants to hang out with. These are people who can ruin his reputation in an instant.

Jesus knows he's being judged and publicly shamed for spending time with them. But he doesn't care about the gossip, he just cares about the people. It's also beautiful to reflect on the fact that outcasts are obviously so comfortable being around Jesus. They're drawn to him, and want to be near him. This means he clearly isn't being judgmental towards them, and he isn't making them feel ashamed, or acting like he's superior to them. He's welcoming, and kind, and warm. This doesn't mean he's approving of their sinful choices, but he is accepting them as people and friends. Can the same be said about you? Do people who are on the fringes of society feel safe with you? Do people who are looked down on by traditional religious folk feel welcomed by you? Do lonely people want to be around you because you so obviously care about them? What about your church? Could a prostitute or an addict or an ex-con or a Muslim refugee or a trans person or a single teen mom or a homeless person walk into your church and feel warmly welcomed in?

The local religious leaders are really unhappy about this dinner party. Jesus is a rabbi, and they think he's a disgrace! He's meant to be a community leader and a good role model. Instead, he's hanging out with a bunch of outcasts, traitors, and criminals. When they openly question his decisions, Jesus replies in verse 17 with some of the most beautifully encouraging words ever spoken: "It is not the healthy who need a doctor, but the sick. I have not come to call the righteous, but sinners." Jesus isn't saying that there are some people who do need saving and some who don't. We're *all* sinners, with no exceptions. We know that from hundreds of other verses in the Bible (including Jesus' own words). So, what exactly is Jesus saying here?

Imagine that there are two women with a very serious disease. The first woman knows she won't survive without a specialist doctor providing her with an accurate diagnosis and appropriate treatment. So she goes to a doctor and the doctor performs the life-saving surgery she needs! The second person's disease is just as serious, but she doesn't want to admit how hopeless her situation is. She feels like it's weak and shameful to acknowledge that she's sick, and she's pretty sure she can fix herself if she tries hard enough. So she carries on with daily life like normal, pretending to herself and everyone else that she's perfectly fine. Unfortunately, her disease *will* eventually kill her. Both women are just as sick as each other. Neither of them can do anything to help themselves. But only one of them was humble enough to ask for help from someone with the skills to save them. Only one of them was willing to even admit they were sick.

Spiritually, we are all like those terminally ill women. The Bible tells us we're all hopeless sinners with no chance of saving ourselves. But the best news in the world is for those of us who desperately know we need help: Jesus came for sinners. Do you know that you're spiritually sick? Then Jesus is ready and waiting to heal you. Do you know that there's nothing you can do to rescue yourself? Then Jesus is holding his hand out to you, saying "Follow me." Are you painfully aware that you are completely and utterly lost on your own? Then take heart, Jesus is calling your name, offering you his free gift of life.

Reflect and respond

1. *What thoughts and feelings go through your mind when you hear that you're a hopeless sinner who needs saving? Why do you feel that way?*
2. *Why do you think 'sinners' clearly feel so comfortable in Jesus' presence? What is it about his character that makes them want to be close to him?*
3. *Think about the outsiders in your community. Do they feel welcomed and safe around you? How can you be more like Jesus to them?*

Merciful God,
Jesus knew that Levi was a dishonest traitor, and he still invited him to be a disciple.
Jesus even knew that Judas would betray him to be killed, and he still invited him to be a disciple.
Thank you that you know everything about me, and you still invite me to be your disciple.
I'm in awe that you go out of your way to love the unlovable, and to forgive shameful, hopeless sinners.
As I spend time with you every day, please teach me how desperately I need you.
Please transform me from the inside out, and use my life to honor you!

In Jesus name,
Amen

Meditation verse for the day:

But God demonstrates his own love for us in this: while we were still sinners, Christ died for us.
(Romans 5:8)

Day 9

Keeping the Sabbath Holy

(READ MARK 2:18–3:6)

IN THIS PASSAGE THE Pharisees accuse Jesus of repeatedly breaking the Jewish religious laws about the Sabbath. Before we focus on the details, let's make sure we're clear on who the Pharisees were, and what the Sabbath means. Pharisees were a group of religious leaders who were very passionate about their Jewish identity and traditions. They worked hard to make sure regular Jewish people were following the laws God gave to Moses, and to help with this they had their own long lists of rules to follow that covered every part of daily life. It's easy to think of them as the bad guys in the Gospels, but actually they were just very zealous men who were defensive against anything they felt threatened their traditional, uniquely Jewish way of life—including Jesus. The Sabbath is what we usually think of as Sunday, the day we go to church. For Jewish people back then and today, the Sabbath lasts from sunset on Friday to sunset on Saturday. The first Christians changed the Sabbath to Sunday in honor of the day of the week Jesus rose from the dead.

The Sabbath

In the Ten Commandments given to Moses in Deuteronomy 5, God commands his people to "remember the Sabbath day by keeping it holy" (verse 12). God says that no work should be done on the Sabbath so that it's a day of rest—a special day set apart for holiness. It's also a day for remembering what God has done for us, celebrating the freedom and salvation that he's freely given us. So the Sabbath is meant to be a day of joyful gratitude, of deep rest and spiritual refreshment, and of reflecting on how great God is. Unfortunately, in a misguided attempt to honor God's command, the religious leaders had made up a huge list of things Jewish people weren't allowed to do on the Sabbath, including carrying things and walking more than a certain distance. The Pharisees treated the Sabbath like a strict rule, but it's actually a beautiful gift from God for us to enjoy. This is what Jesus means in verse 27 when he says, "The Sabbath was made for man, not man for the Sabbath." He's reminding the Pharisees that God meant for the Sabbath to be a refreshing, life-giving day for his people. He's explaining that God actually created the Sabbath as a blessing for us!

The law or the gospel?

Through this conflict with the Pharisees over the Sabbath, Jesus is showing us that there are two very different ways to approach our relationship with God. The way of the Pharisees is to try and do all the right things so that God will approve of them. This kind of attitude is called 'self-righteousness'. They're so obsessed with keeping lists of rules that they're missing opportunities to show mercy and bring healing to others. Jesus is so sad about their cold, unloving attitudes, because it's so far from God's true heart for the Sabbath.

Jesus invites us to relate to God in a completely different way. He has already done everything necessary for God to be pleased with us. He says that nothing we do could ever make God love us any more or any less, because God's love isn't based on us at all! It's based on Jesus and what he has already done on the cross. This sets us free from having to strive to prove ourselves to God. The Bible calls this 'grace': the unearned gift of God's love. All we need to do is receive it, by turning to God in faith and trusting him to save us. Stop here for a moment and let that sink in. God loves you so much right this second, that it's impossible for him to ever love you more. He loves you perfectly, completely, wholly, tenderly, wonderfully! He adores you, cherishes you, and delights in you. He will never love you any less, no matter what.

No. Matter. What.

Why? Because his love for you isn't based on who you are, or what you've done, or whether you're worthy of it. You didn't earn it in the first place, so you can't lose it. No wonder they call it amazing grace! God's grace sets us free.

Obeying God's law is still important for Christians, but we obey with a totally different motivation than self-righteous religious people. They obey out of fear and pride, seeing obedience as a way to earn God's approval. But we obey him because we trust that his wise ways are the best thing for us. We obey because we want to be more like our Father, and his laws teach us what he's like. And we obey knowing that no matter how many times we mess it all up, God's love for us doesn't change one single bit.

Your Sabbath

So what should the Sabbath mean for us today? We live in a culture that's addicted to being busy. We hurry everywhere we go, scheduling activities into every moment of every day and racing between them without stopping to take a breath. We never stop striving to prove ourselves. We think our self-worth comes from what we do. Our spirits are constantly anxious and overwhelmed, and we feel like we're never doing enough, and never achieving enough. We sit with people we love but don't give them our full attention, because we're distracted by our phones. We pride ourselves on working hard and playing harder, and then wonder why we feel burnt out. We're exhausted but can't fall asleep at night because our minds just won't stop racing. We talk a lot about self-care, but the statistics show that young people these days are more anxious and depressed and stressed out than any humans have ever been in history! We really struggle to slow down and make space to sit quietly with God. No wonder our wise and loving God has commanded us to take Sabbath rest very seriously! He really does know what our souls need most. If you would like to think more deeply about resting well, Pastor John Mark Comer has a fantastic book called *The Ruthless Elimination of Hurry*, which includes an entire chapter on the Sabbath.

So what should you do on the Sabbath to keep it holy? The beauty of Jesus' response to the Pharisees is that he's giving us great freedom in how to do it. Followers of Jesus aren't limited by the restrictive rules of the Pharisees! In fact, in Matthew 11:28 Jesus promises, "Come to me, all you who are weary and burdened, and I will give you rest." *He* is where we find rest. *In his presence* is where we're refreshed and renewed and encouraged. So really the only question is: How can you practice coming closer to Jesus on your Sabbath? How can you spend your day basking in his presence?

If nature helps you focus on the majesty and creativity of God, maybe you could spend time by the ocean or in the mountains or out in your garden. Quality time with your friends and family might encourage you to remember God's goodness. Or perhaps you enjoy celebrating God's wonderful gifts to you by cooking or eating a delicious meal. Worshipping God together with our church community is always a special and important way to draw nearer to Jesus. Whatever you choose to do on your Sabbath, make sure God is at the center of it. Turn your phone off so that the outside world doesn't steal your attention away. Make time for stillness and quiet and solitude with God. Read your Bible and pray. Talk to him, listen to him, enjoy him. Sing of his goodness. Remember and celebrate his kindness in all the little miracles that surround you. And if you get to bring healing and peace to others on the Sabbath, joyfully take those opportunities, just like Jesus did.

Reflect and respond

1. *Think about some of God's laws that you struggle to understand or obey. How might it help you to think about those laws as a wise gift from God that he designed for your good?*
2. *Reflect on the description of God's grace above. How does grace set you free?*
3. *What restful, worshipful activities could you do on your Sabbath to practice enjoying God more?*

God of grace,
Thank you for your grace and love.
I could never earn it. I don't deserve it.
It's all a free gift from you, and I am so grateful.
You are so kind to me!
I'm so grateful that I don't have to be like the Pharisees, striving to be as good as possible every day to earn your love.
I'm also grateful that I don't have to be like the world, working so hard to achieve success and burning myself out to prove I have worth.
Thank you for offering me the gift of true rest in Jesus.
Help me learn to Sabbath well, so that I can slow down and deeply enjoy you and your good gifts.
I want you to be my rest and my delight!

In Jesus name,
Amen

Meditation verse for the day:

The Sabbath was made for man,
not man for the Sabbath.
(Mark 2:27)

Day 10

The Twelve Disciples

(Read Mark 3:7-19)

As you read this passage, put yourself in Jesus' shoes for a moment. He's trying to get away for a while with his closest followers, but just can't escape the crowds. They're coming to him from all over the countryside, gathering around him in huge groups, desperate for a miracle, pushing against each other to reach him. It would have been chaotic and stressful. These crowds aren't there to listen to what Jesus has to say, or because they want to get to know him better. They aren't interested in becoming disciples. They've just heard that he can fix their problems.

There are so many times that we treat God in exactly the same way as this crowd treated Jesus. We forget about God completely until we have a problem that we need fixed. We don't pray much when everything is going well in our lives, only when disaster strikes. But these verses show us a lot about the mercy and love of God. See how Jesus graciously heals the sick people and casts out demons! He doesn't owe these people anything, and yet he willingly sacrifices his own time and energy, inconveniencing himself to meet their needs. What a kind God we have.

The twelve disciples

In verses 13-19 Jesus finally manages to get away from the huge crowd. Up on a lonely mountain, he handpicks twelve very interesting people to be his closest disciples. You might expect Jesus to strategically pick people who are going to be able to help his ministry be successful, like powerful or rich people. Instead, Jesus mostly picks fishermen. These guys are pretty uneducated and relatively poor, which makes them a surprising choice. In fact, as we read more about the twelve disciples we'll see that they were actually quite an average bunch, who didn't even understand half the stuff Jesus said to them. They argued amongst themselves. They let Jesus down over and over again, and abandoned him completely when he needed them most. Peter denied he even knew Jesus. James and John were called the Sons of Thunder because they were fiercely bold and reckless when they got angry. Judas would even betray Jesus to be killed. Jesus knew all that, and yet he still chose them and invited them to do life with him. I love how pastor Eugene Peterson describes this: "Any time we target our invitations to the people we assume are especially useful to the kingdom—the prominent, the wealthy, men and women with proven leadership abilities and skills that can benefit the kingdom, we are ignoring the way Jesus went about it... He said "Follow me," and ended up with a bunch of losers. And these losers ended up, through no virtue or talent of their own, becoming saints. Jesus wasn't after the best but the worst. He came to seek and save the lost." So if you've ever felt like a loser, take heart!

Choosing to use very ordinary and unlikely people is actually the way God has been working the whole way through human history. Read the Old Testament and you'll see it time and time again. God always picks the youngest brother, the ugly sister, the women who can't have children, the man with a stutter, the prostitute, the fearful coward, the foreigner, the poor widow. He fights on the side of weak Israel against powerful Egypt, and little David against huge Goliath. He chooses the foolish to teach the wise. The reason why God acts like this is explained in 2 Corinthians 4:7: "But we have this treasure in jars of clay to show that this all-surpassing power is from God and not from us." This means that we're like weak, cracked clay jars holding a wondrous treasure. Our weakness and ordinariness is exactly why God loves to use us in his story, because it draws attention to *him*, not to us. Any strength we have is obviously his strength. Any success we have is a gift from him. Anything we achieve is him working through us. There can be no other earthly explanation when losers become saints.

Unity in the church

Two disciples from the list are particularly interesting: Matthew the tax collector and Simon the Zealot. As we read about a few days ago, the Jewish people had been conquered and were living under Roman occupation. This meant that Rome had complete control of their land and their towns, and ruled over most aspects of their daily lives. The Jews understandably hated this, and they responded to the oppression in different ways. People like the tax collectors chose to work for the Roman government and got rich by working against their own people. The Zealots were the exact opposite: They were violent Jewish nationalists who fought against the rule of the Romans every chance they got. They were ready to die for their freedom, regularly leading bloody uprisings against the much stronger Roman army. That's why it's so surprising that Jesus' disciples included both a tax collector and a zealot! It's hard to imagine people who might struggle to get along more. And yet they were somehow brought together by following Jesus.

This is a beautiful picture of what Christians should be like. The world encourages us to judge people who aren't like us. But Jesus says in John 13:35 that his disciples should stand out by the way that we love each other. That doesn't mean we all agree all the time, or that we all have similar personalities or identical political beliefs or speak the same language. It means that following Jesus brings us together regardless of any other differences we have. Following Jesus is the most important part of our identities; more important than our cultural heritage, political beliefs, age, gender, bank balance, or skin color. And following Jesus unites us with other Christians in a deep and holy way that goes against anything the world understands. Heaven will be made up of people from every tribe and language and nation, all singing together with one heart! Until then, we have the opportunity to be heaven on earth, by being a community that welcomes and embraces everyone, no matter how different they might be from us. Church should be a safe place where we can humbly learn from each other and lovingly grow together to be more like Jesus. So look around you at your friends and the people in your church. Do they all look like you? Vote like you? Talk like you? Have the same amount of money as you? Or does your community look more like a reflection of heaven, filled with a supernaturally beautiful unity in diversity?

Reflect and respond

1. What part of today's devotions challenged you the most, and why?
2. What is something from today's devotions that you're thankful for?

Lord God,
It's so encouraging that you're merciful towards people who don't deserve it.
I'm in awe that you choose to use ordinary people like the disciples and me to give the world the good news of your kingdom.
You bring together natural enemies and unite us in peace and love.
God, please use my messy, broken life to show off your greatness.
Holy Spirit, teach me how to love radically, so that everyone knows I'm a Christian.

In Jesus name,
Amen

Meditation verse for the day:

But God chose the foolish things of the world
to shame the wise;
God chose the weak things of the world
to shame the strong.
God chose the lowly things of this world
and the despised things . . .
so that no one may boast before him.
(1 Corinthians 1:27–29)

Day 11

The Eternal Sin

(Read Mark 3:20–35)

Jesus is being attacked from every side. He's simply trying to sit down to eat a quiet meal, but desperate crowds are still demanding miracles. As usual, the religious leaders are looking for ways to challenge his authority. And his own family are embarrassed by him and think he's had a breakdown. It must have hurt Jesus to hear that his own family didn't have his back. He probably felt quite discouraged and lonely. Maybe you have personal experience of being misunderstood by the people who should know and love you best. Jesus understands your pain.

Repentance

Let's focus our attention on verses 28 and 29, which are the most difficult verses in this passage. Jesus starts verse 28 by saying that "people can be forgiven for all their sins and every slander they utter." How encouraging! Jesus uses very inclusive language here; "all" and "every" cover pretty much everything you could think of. This is exactly what the entire Bible teaches about forgiveness. Everyone from the Old Testament prophets, to John the Baptist, to Jesus himself, to the leaders of the earliest Christian churches all preach that if we repent, he'll forgive us. End of story. No exceptions.

This is the most glorious news in the world! Hallelujah! There is literally nothing you could think or do or say that's so bad that God will not forgive you if you repent. But that's the key right there: *if you repent*. Repenting means turning our hearts away from our sin, and turning back to God. All the way through the Bible we consistently see that there's no hope of forgiveness without humble repentance. But God never, ever holds back his forgiveness from people who are genuinely sorry. There will often still be natural consequences for our bad choices, but God loves to forgive his children when we see that we're on the wrong path and turn back to him. He longs to be in a right relationship with us.

Blaspheming the Holy Spirit

Since Jesus has just reminded us that we can be forgiven for every and any sin, verse 29 can seem a bit confusing: "But whoever blasphemes against the Holy Spirit will never be forgiven; they are guilty of an eternal sin." Is Jesus contradicting himself? He's just said *all* sins can be forgiven, and now he's saying that there actually is one sin that will *never* be forgiven.

To understand what Jesus means here, we need to remember that the requirement for forgiveness is repentance. God only forgives people who repent. So 'blaspheming the Holy Spirit' must be another way of saying 'not repenting.' One of the Holy Spirit's jobs is to help us see how sinful we are. He also changes our hearts to want to turn back to God—without him we are so sinful we can't even choose to believe in Jesus! So without the Holy Spirit, we could never be saved. But all the way through the Bible we also learn that even though God calls us to himself and makes us able to respond to his call, we're still personally responsible for how we choose to respond to him. God never forces us to repent. He doesn't make us love him. We can actually choose to ignore the work of the Holy Spirit in our hearts. We can choose to run away from God when he calls us. We can choose to hate God and to love our sin instead. We can reject the Holy Spirit's gifts of conviction and repentance and faith.

So this is what Jesus means when he talks about blaspheming the Holy Spirit. God wants to forgive every single person on earth. He longs for us to turn back to him and to let him love us. But if we spend our lives resisting the Holy Spirit's conviction, ignoring the Holy Spirit's guidance, and rejecting the things he teaches us about God, we're going to miss the opportunity to repent. And if we don't repent, we can't be forgiven.

So what does this mean for me today?

If you're terrified that your sins are unforgiveable, remember the context of this passage. Jesus started by saying that God loves to forgive all and any sins that we repent for. Even that sin that you just keep stumbling over time and time again. This passage is a warning to people like the Pharisees and the teachers of the law, who know God's word and hear God's voice and see God's character, but keep on rejecting Jesus anyway. If you know you're a sinner today, it's because the Holy Spirit is opening your eyes to be able to see your sin for what it is. If you want to get to know God better today, it's because the Holy Spirit is gently working in your heart, inviting you to draw closer to God. Don't block out his voice today. Don't reject him. Don't harden your heart against his loving guidance. Listen to him, and he will lead you to forgiveness and life.

Reflect and respond

1. Reflect on the role of God the Spirit in the lives of Christians. How have you seen the Holy Spirit at work in your own heart recently?
2. God promises to forgive anyone who repents of their sin. What does that mean to you personally?

God of mercy,
You promise that if I repent and return to you, you will forgive me.
You promise that if I turn from my sin, you'll be gracious and merciful.
Please forgive me.
Please help me hate my sin and love you instead.
Thank you that even when I'm faithless, you are faithful.
Thank you for gently drawing me to yourself with the gift of your Holy Spirit.
Please give me a humble heart.
Help me listen to your voice and respond in repentance and faith.

In Jesus name,
Amen

The Eternal Sin

Meditation verse for the day:

If we confess our sins, he is faithful and just
and will forgive us our sins
and purify us from all unrighteousness.
(1 John 1:9)

Day 12

The Parable of the Sower—Part 1

(READ MARK 4:1–20)

IN THIS PARABLE, JESUS explains the different ways people respond to the message of the Bible. As we study this parable over the next two days, prayerfully think about which type of ground is closest to your own personal response to God's truth.

The path

Jesus says that the seed in this story symbolizes the Bible: the words of God written to us! The first place the seed is scattered is the path. Jesus explains in verse 15 that the path represents people who hear the word of God but it goes in one ear and out the other. They're physically in a place where they can hear the truth about God, but it never makes it to their hearts.

Be honest: How often do you sit in church with your mind focused on something else? Or maybe you read quickly through your devotions every morning, but then it makes absolutely no difference to how you go about your day. The words were literally in front of your eyes, but left absolutely no footprint on your soul or life. Jesus is saying that we can have his words in our ears and still not ever really hear him. We can be around his truth without it having any effect on us. We can go to church seven days a week and read the Bible for hours a day, but it won't make a single bit of difference in our lives if we don't listen thoughtfully or prayerfully reflect on what we hear. How we respond is what matters.

The Parable of the Sower—Part 1

The rocky place

The second type of person Jesus describes is someone who starts out eager to hear God's word, but it doesn't go deep enough into their hearts and minds to grow any roots (verses 5 and 6). They feel enthusiastic about God and being a Christian, until hard times come. Then they lose their passion for God and give up walking with him. It's one thing to feel excited about God's love and wisdom when life's all going well, but what we really believe is usually only revealed when we're suffering. When our hearts are breaking, do we still trust that God is good? When the disappointment is almost too much to bear, will we still worship him? When we're stuck and can't see a way out, do we have peace knowing that God is still in control? When people hate us, can we rest knowing that our identity comes from God? When we've lost everything we love, are we content that God really is enough for us? Often we have no idea what we actually believe is true about God until hard times come. As much as it hurts, those hard experiences show us what's really deep inside ourselves.

Suffering is never easy. We all have doubts, we all lose faith sometimes, and we all have times where we struggle to feel God's presence. Suffering is a natural part of being human in a sinful world, and unfortunately that isn't going to change until heaven. But that's exactly why it's so important to have deep, healthy spiritual roots. Our roots are how we survive the storms and droughts of life. Not because our roots are so strong, but because our roots connect us to Jesus, who is strong. Our roots are how we're able to soak up the life that Jesus offers us in himself. Our roots channel his grace and mercy into our lives. When we're deeply rooted in God, he sustains us and steadies us and holds us firm, no matter what's happening around us. Suffering *will* happen to you. Are you prepared to suffer well?

The thorns

The third type of response Jesus describes is represented by the thorny ground. These people hear the word of God and it starts to make a difference inside them, but it never ends up bearing any fruit in their lives. In verse 19 Jesus explains that this lack of any real growth is because the little seed gets smothered by "the worries of this life, the deceitfulness of wealth and the desires for other things." These people spend so much time thinking about themselves, obsessing over what they want to achieve in life and stressing about how to get it all, that there isn't enough space left in their hearts for God's word to really grow. Jesus isn't saying that it's wrong to have hopes and dreams for the future. He's warning us that the devil will try to seduce us with promises of the good life. He distracts us with careers and binge-watching the latest season of another TV show. He tempts us to long for material stuff and worldly success more than we long for intimacy with our heavenly Father. Jesus warns us strongly against having these priorities: "What good is it for someone to gain the whole world, yet forfeit their soul?" (Mark 8:36).

In our materialistic, workaholic, anxious world, I think this response is the most natural and dangerous one for most of us. It's very easy to genuinely love Jesus but spend most of our hours every day distracted by other stuff. Think through your last week. How much time did you spend enjoying God's presence, or meditating on his word, or worshiping him, or talking about him with your friends? Compare that with how much time you spent stressed out, or working hard so that you pass that test, or win that game, or perform well enough that you can prove yourself and not feel like a failure. And then add in how much time you spent daydreaming about stuff you want, or browsing online the things you want to buy soon, or talking about the stuff you want with your friends. How much time do you spend scrolling on your phone looking at the lives of influencers and celebrities and gamers, wishing you had what they had? How many TV shows or movies did you spend hours in front of, longing for that romance or that lifestyle or that wardrobe to be your own? We are at risk of distracting ourselves to death! As pastor John Mark Comer says, "How we spend our time is how we spend our lives. It's who we become (or don't become)."[1] How do you spend your time? Who are you becoming? What fruit is your life bearing?

The word of life

Let's be really clear about one thing: Jesus isn't saying here that we're saved or not saved depending on how carefully we read the Bible. Our salvation doesn't depend on how hard we try to understand. The Bible itself doesn't save us. The strength of our faith doesn't save us. Our spiritual roots don't save us. *God saves us.*

However, even though the Bible doesn't save us, it *is* absolutely essential to how we become mature, healthy, flourishing Christians. The Bible

---

1. Comer, *Elimination of Hurry*, 72.

is the main way God speaks to us. Through the words of the Bible, we're introduced to God. The Bible is where we discover the truth that sets us free. It provides us with a firm foundation so we're not led astray by false teachers or by the seductive lies of our culture. It's the sword of the Spirit, our powerful weapon against the attacks of Satan. The Bible is a central way God floods our lives with his grace and power. Jesus is warning us in this parable that we would be extremely foolish to treat his word lightly, and not to give it our full attention. So whether you read a physical Bible, read the Bible on your phone, or listen to an audio version of the Bible, make sure you're spending time in the word every single day! Approach it with the reverence and thoughtfulness it deserves. Pray that God will give you ears to really hear, and a heart to really respond.

Reflect and respond

1. *In what ways are you like the path? How does Satan distract you so that God's word goes in one ear and out the other?*
2. *In what ways are you like the rocky ground? How do hard times threaten your trust in God?*
3. *In what ways are you like the thorny ground? What worries or desires clog up your heart and mind so that there's no room left for growing deeper with Jesus?*

Lord,
Thank you for your precious word.
I am so grateful that you've given me the Bible so that I can learn about who you are, and who you created me to be. Help me to love your word, and to meditate on it every day so that your truth becomes deeply rooted in my heart and mind.
I want to listen well, but I find it so hard to focus.
Give me ears to really hear and understand you.
I want to build my life on you, my firm foundation.
I want to grow deep roots in you, the river of living water.

In Jesus name,
Amen

Meditation verse for the day:

The law of the Lord is perfect,
refreshing the soul . . .
The commands of the Lord are radiant,
giving light to the eyes.
(Psalm 19:7–8)

Day 13

The Parable of the Sower—Part 2

(Read Mark 4:1–20)

The good soil

Today we're going to finish Jesus' parable about listening well to God's word. In verse 8 Jesus says that the good soil represents the response of people who hear God's word, accept it, and live fruitful lives as a result. But what does it mean to really *accept* God's word in a way that changes us? Anyone can study the words of the Bible, and know all the right things about God. The Pharisees did that very well. They even had huge sections of the Old Testament completely memorized! But Jesus wants us to go much deeper, by really believing that the words in the Bible are true and good and beautiful. He wants us to build every part of our lives on who God says he is. Accepting his word means to treat the Bible like it's actually God himself speaking to us, and to give his words the authority to challenge and shape every part of our lives. Accepting it means letting scripture become a part of us, forming us from the inside out. Accepting it means living what we read. Psalm 1 puts the message of this parable into different words:

> "Blessed is the one... whose delight is in the law of the Lord, and who meditates on his law day and night. That person is like a tree planted by streams of water, which yields its fruit in its season, and whose leaf does not wither" (Ps 1:1–3).

We all want a faith like this, right? We want to be like beautiful trees, radiant with flowers and fruit and lush green leaves. We want to overflow with joy and inner strength, flourishing and thriving in our deepest hearts! But just like the healthy tree needs the constant stream of fresh water, the psalmist says our souls need regular nourishment from God's word. Spiritually feeding on the Bible means meditating on it and loving it. It means taking it into the deepest parts of ourselves and living out of it. It means letting the Bible shape who we are becoming. Not because the words in the Bible are somehow magic, but because God has chosen to use words as the main channel for his grace to pour into our lives. With the Holy Spirit's help, the words of the Bible come alive and are streams of water to our souls, refreshing us and sustaining us and forming us to be more like Jesus.

There is a wonderful promise hidden in this parable. In verse 20, Jesus says that those who listen and embrace his word, will "produce a harvest beyond their wildest dreams" (MSG). When Jesus talks about harvests and fruitfulness, he means growing in our own personal holiness, as well as learning to love God and our neighbors better, and having the joy of inviting others into the kingdom of God. What a breath-taking vision for your life! Jesus doesn't only want you to have a healthy faith because it's what is best for you. He's *much* more generous than that. He wants to give you an abundance of love so that it can overflow to the people around you. He wants to pour out his goodness and mercy and kindness on you, so that you can pour it out on others. He invites you to be the little seed he uses to transform your family and community. The Holy Spirit can use your life to bring more joy and hope and healing to the people around you than you ever dreamed was possible! As Jesus beautifully says in John 7:38, "Whoever believes in me, as Scripture has said, rivers of living water will flow from within them." Don't you long to be a river of living water to the hurting world around you? Wouldn't you like to be the sort of person who spreads love and joy and peace? Jesus wants to build you up into a person who refreshes the hearts of others everywhere you go. It's what you were made for!

Spiritual reading

Good soil doesn't just happen by accident. We need to be deliberate about making sure we are good soil for the seeds of God's word. But how do we do this? Pastor Eugene Peterson recommends an ancient way of reading the Bible called *lectio divina* or 'spiritual reading', which he describes as "reading that enters our souls as food enters our stomachs, spreads through our blood, and becomes holiness and love and wisdom."[1] Spiritual reading is not a study technique, it's about making space for the Holy Spirit to use God's words to transform us from the inside out. "It is a cultivated, developed habit of *living* the text in Jesus' name."[2] Here is how Peterson suggests we feed our souls on the Bible every day:

1. *Read.* Set aside quality time to read the Bible at the start of every day. Be intentional about identifying things that distract you, and get away from them. Turn off your phone. Get enough sleep at night so that you can focus properly. Be disciplined with your time. Find a quiet place for your devotions so that you won't be interrupted. Reading is a skill, and the Bible is filled with poetry and metaphors, history and biographies, narrative and prophecies. Because of this, we can't interpret each book of the Bible in the exact same way, so find trustworthy mentors and helpful books to guide you in how to read each different type of literature in the Bible. I really love the *God's Word For You* commentary series, which goes through each book one verse at a time.

2. *Meditate.* Differently from some other types of meditation, Christian meditation means to deliberately practice remembering God's words throughout the day. That might mean reflecting on a Bible verse or memorizing Scripture during any free time you have, like walking between classes, driving to work, or waiting for the bus. Meditation is where we deliberately build connections between God's voice and the places and relationships where we live out our faith. Have you ever got to the end of the day and completely forgotten what you read in your morning devotions? We all do that. But by meditating regularly on the Bible, we give our morning devotions a chance to seep out into the rest of our day. The famous minister Martyn Lloyd-Jones once wrote, "Have you realized that most of your unhappiness in life is due to the fact that you are listening to yourself instead of talking to yourself? . . . Remind yourself of God, who God is, and what God is and what God has done, and what God has pledged himself to do."[3] Lloyd-Jones encourages us to preach to ourselves what the Bible says, day in and day

---

1. Peterson, *Eat This Book*, 4.
2. Peterson, *Eat This Book*, 116.
3. Lloyd-Jones, *Spiritual Depression*, 20–21.

out. I like to literally speak God's truths out loud to myself through my day. Preaching God's word to ourselves is how we bring what we've read into our actual lives.

3. *Pray.* God speaks to us in the Bible, but he wants a two-way conversation with us. Prayer is how we answer. Prayer is how we participate. This is why the book of Psalms is in the Bible: to teach us how to pray! The psalms show us that prayer can be songs or poetry, sobs or silence. In the psalms we see people bringing every single human emotion to God in prayer. The psalms teach us that some prayers are prayed in groups, and some are prayed in the loneliest solitude. The psalms teach us how to pray the Bible back to God, saying: "This is who you say you are, God. This is what you've promised. This is how much you say you love me. Be who you say you are to me." Jesus quoted the psalms more than anything else, and probably knew all the psalms off by heart. Christians throughout history have regularly sung and prayed the psalms. They teach us how to talk to God about every single part of life. So pray the psalms. Pray the words of your devotions, making them your own. Pray your honest thoughts and feelings. Pray your whole life out to God.

4. *Live the text.* Go into the world and live out what you've read and prayed. "There is no word of God that God does not intend to be lived by us."[4] Live it in your home and in your school and in your workplace, in your family and in your friendships and in your romances. This isn't a spiritual requirement or a rule; it's a natural outpouring of Christ in us, an overflow of everything we've read and meditated on and prayed through. We live the text by receiving the grace God has for us, moment by moment. We live the text by loving the Lord our God with all our hearts and souls and minds, and by loving our neighbors as ourselves. We live the text by resting in who God is and who he's made us to be. We live the text by remembering that we are citizens of the kingdom of God, even now.

Let God's words nourish and nurture you, and you will be good soil. You will be a tree planted by streams of water. You will live a wondrously fruitful life, wildly beyond anything you could have imagined or hoped for. You will find yourself growing in love, joy, peace, patience, kindness, goodness, faithfulness, gentleness, and self-control. But always remember

---

4. Peterson, *Eat This Book*, 114.

that discipleship is not something you do by yourself. All the through the Bible we see the importance of God's people gathering to study God's word together, encourage one another, and hold each other accountable. So go to church and Bible study groups regularly. Talk about your Bible readings with your Christian friends and family. Meet up with a friend or mentor every week to talk about what God is teaching you in his word. Once you start feeding on the Bible in this way, you will never be the same again.

Reflect and respond

1. What does Jesus' promise of fruitfulness mean to you? How does it reflect your deepest longings for your life?
2. What are two new ways you can cultivate a listening heart and mind, so that you are good soil?

Most High God,
Please make these words from Psalm 119 the desire of my heart today:
Open my eyes so that I can see wonderful things in your word.
Help me understand your ways, so that I can meditate on your wonderful deeds.
Be gracious to me and teach me your commands.
Give me understanding so that I may keep your law and obey it with all my heart.
Turn my heart towards your truths and turn my eyes away from worthless things.
The law from your mouth is more precious to me than silver and gold.
Your word, Lord, is eternal; it stands firm in the heavens.
Your word is a lamp for my feet, and a light on my path.

In Jesus' name,
Amen

Meditation verse for the day:

Blessed is the one who trusts in the Lord,
whose confidence is in him.
They will be like a tree planted by the water
that sends out its roots by the stream.
It does not fear when heat comes;
its leaves are always green.
It has no worries in a year of drought
and never fails to bear fruit.
(Jeremiah 17:7–8)

Day 14

The King and His Kingdom

(Read Mark 4:21–41)

The kingdom of God

In two of his parables today, Jesus describes the kingdom of God. Remember that God's kingdom is not a country or a place, but a way of describing God's spiritual reign as Lord and King. Anyone who's a Christian, at any time in history, in any part of the world, speaking any language, belongs to the kingdom of God. It's Jesus' favourite topic—he talks about it all the time!

So what is he teaching us here about the kingdom of God? Both of these parables use the metaphors of seeds again. Seeds are very small, very unimpressive, and very easy to underestimate. They aren't anything special to look at, and they don't seem very powerful. But when they're planted in good soil, seeds transform into something brand new and totally incredible! They grow almost miraculously, sprouting deep underground and eventually growing into something much, much bigger than you would ever expect.

These parables teach us a stunning truth. Jesus is reminding us that God isn't the kind of king we would expect from someone so powerful and majestic and holy. He could force everyone to bow before him as master, but he lovingly chooses not to use his unlimited power over us like that. He never hits us over the head with his right to be our Lord. Instead, the

Almighty God comes to us gently and softly. He speaks to us in tenderness and intimacy. He humbly lowers himself down to our level. He kindly welcomes the lost and the sinners, the rejects and the outcasts and the weak. He invites us to listen to him, and to trust him. He even gives us the option of rejecting him! He pursues a real relationship with us. He wants us to get to know him the way he knows us. He loves us, adores us, and cherishes us. Just let that amaze you for a moment. What a God!

If you've ever felt like this world is a huge mess, then God's up-side-down kingdom is the home you've been searching for. In a world that celebrates winning at all costs, the kingdom of God is soft and gentle. In a world obsessed with power and wealth, Christianity started with a humble carpenter and some fishermen. In a world where everyone wants to be a famous celebrity, the Lord of lords had just twelve ordinary disciples who he sang with and fished with and cried with and ate with and loved. In a world that says we need to fight for political power to control our enemies and protect ourselves, Jesus chooses to avoid power altogether and just spend his life with the people on the bottom rung of society. He died a shameful, humiliating death, sacrificing himself for you and for me. But just like the tiny seeds in the parables, his small, quiet revolution is still wonderfully alive today, all around the world. The name of Jesus is worshipped in different languages across the globe, by young and by old, by rich and by poor. God is still working beneath the surface, and his kingdom is still growing, and he's still transforming lives this very moment, bringing unimaginable hope and joy and rest for tired souls. His kingdom is like nothing the world has ever seen before. Is his kingdom your home?

Jesus calms the storm

Today's passage ends with the very famous story of Jesus calming a storm. The disciples have spent their lives on boats, but they're freaking out! They really believe they're not going to make it out of this storm alive, and they let their panic overwhelm them. In complete contrast, Jesus is comfortably curled up with a cosy cushion, fast asleep. This is such a beautiful picture of the way that deep intimacy with God changes how we experience hard times in life. The disciples have walked with Jesus for a while now, but they still don't really know the full story of who he is; in verse 41 they're looking at each other asking, "Who *is* this guy?!" Because they don't understand him, the storm fills them with fear. On the other hand, Jesus has spent all eternity knowing and loving and trusting God his Father. He knows that he's beloved by the God who spoke all of creation into existence. God's words are written on his heart. God's Spirit lives in him and empowers everything he does. So, in spite of the frightening waves crashing into the boat all around him, he's able to rest peacefully.

The Bible never tells us that once we're walking with Jesus, life will be easy. Remember, even Jesus himself was led into the dangerous wilderness, and he ended up being violently killed. The Bible doesn't say that God will calm all of our storms, even though he can. Instead, the Bible promises that when our lives are deeply rooted in God, storms don't need to scare us anymore. Fear doesn't need to overwhelm us. Instead, we can rest. We can have peaceful hearts in the middle of the greatest suffering because we know that God is with us and for us. We can lie down in bed and sleep well, instead of letting our anxieties and fears race through our minds all night long. We can trust that our Father is good, and that he loves us, and that he's in control of the storms that are threatening our lives.

No matter how many times you've heard this story, please read verse 39 again and picture this moment in your mind. Imagine the worst storm you've ever experienced. Take a moment to gaze in awe at the power of Jesus here. He easily calms the terrifying waves with just a few words. The natural world recognizes his voice and immediately obeys its maker. Jesus shows that he's in complete control. He's totally sovereign, which means he's totally in charge. Even his own disciples are terrified by the powerful authority he displays in this moment. This is the mighty God we serve. All of creation is his. Hallelujah!

Reflect and respond

1. *What has God shown you about himself today, that makes you feel awe and reverence towards him?*
2. *What kind of hard times have you experienced lately? How do you usually feel when a terrible storm hits your life?*
3. *How can you fight fear the next time a life-storm comes?*

Lord God Almighty,
You reign over all of creation, from the largest galaxies and deepest oceans to the tiniest cell in my body. It all belongs to you.
I praise you that you're in control, and that you're loving and wise.
I surrender everything I am to your lordship.
I want you to be my King, and I want your kingdom to be my home.
This world makes me exhausted, and I need to you be my rest.
The storms around me scare me, and I need you to give me faith.
Show me how to trust you when the hard times come.
Teach me how to rest humbly in your tender love, no matter what's happening around me.

In Jesus name,
Amen

Meditation verse for the day:

God is our refuge and strength,
an ever-present help in trouble.
Therefore we will not fear,
though the earth give way and
the mountains fall into the heart of the sea.
(Psalm 46:1–2)

Day 15

The Demon-Possessed Man

(Read Mark 5:1–20)

In this passage, we're reminded again of the amazing authority of Jesus: Even the demons have no choice but to obey him! And this is not just one demon. When Jesus asks the demon its name in verse 9, it calls itself Legion, "for we are many." A legion was a word from the Roman army, meaning a group of about 5000 soldiers. We're talking about a whole *lot* of demons here!

Jesus, the restorer

The poor man in this passage has no home except a graveyard, and no friends except tombs. He was a lonely outcast living on the edge of society. He's not dressed properly, he's crying out non-stop, and he's cutting himself all over with stones. Local people have tried to chain him up before, maybe for his own safety or maybe because they're scared of him. This is a desperate man who's lost all hope. He's been completely rejected by everyone who has ever known him. He has nothing left. Imagine walking past a man like that on the street. Would you make eye contact? Or would you cross to the other side of the street to avoid having to get too close?

As we've already seen over and over, Jesus loves to restore brokenness. It's his deepest nature to heal, to mend, to bring dead things back to life, and to give hope to the hopeless. He draws the very closest to suffering people. He meets this deeply hurting man right where he is, in the middle of a graveyard, and then completely transforms him. Jesus immediately sets him free from the demons that are destroying his mind and his body, and that have cut him off from other people. After meeting Jesus, this man is a completely new person, with a new story to tell and a new hope for the future! He is restored! His life is changed forever.

Do you realize that this poor, sick man is *you*? Spiritually, you are in exactly the same position before God as he is. Without Jesus, you are just as weak and hopeless and lost. You can't do anything to save yourself. You don't have anything to offer God that he could ever want or need. I'm not saying this to make you feel bad about yourself. It's actually the best news in the world, because Jesus *only* came to seek and save people who know they're lost. It's only when we recognise that we're just as spiritually lost as the man in this story, that we're able to receive the free gift of restoration that Jesus offers us. That's what grace is all about! And this man's experience is exactly what a real encounter with God does for each of us. Jesus always meets us right where we're at, but he never leaves us there. He longs to transform your life, restoring you to wholeness and making you a new creation in him. Our kind God loves to have compassion on the humble, and to show his mercy and power through people the world has given up on. No one is too lost for God.

The spiritual realm

It's tempting to go through life believing that what we see is all there is. This story reminds us that there is a spiritual realm that's very real, and that impacts our lives on this earth. Demons are very real, and very dangerous. They're trying to completely ruin this man, in a deeply humiliating and painful way. The Bible tells us that the devil is always prowling around us like a hungry lion, looking for ways to "steal and kill and destroy" (John 10:10). Demons and evil spirits aren't just imaginary characters from horror movies, and they didn't all disappear thousands of years ago. They can still be a cause of mental illness and other serious health problems, just like they are all the way through the Gospels. Many people from traditional indigenous cultures have a much better understanding of this spiritual realm than those of us from Western cultures. But the Bible tells us very clearly: "Put on all of God's armor so that you will be able to stand firm against all the strategies of the devil. For we are not fighting against flesh-and-blood enemies, but against evil rulers and authorities of the unseen world, against mighty powers in this dark world, and against evil spirits in the heavenly places" (Ephesians 6:11–12, NLT). There's a spiritual battle raging behind the scenes of our physical world, and we need to be prepared for it.

Unfortunately, many people around the world today don't take spiritual things seriously. They happily watch horror movies with occult themes, or dabble in witchcraft, or casually participate in powerful spiritual activities from other religions. For example, I know many people who think it's fun to go to a fortune teller, but it's no joke. Acts 16:16–19 tells us that some people really *can* tell the future, because the demons inside them give them that power. It's very real. But anything spiritual that does not come from God is evil. It's not harmless fun. These demons are not something to play with. They are not weak. They are not entertainment. They're real, and they're trying to find a way into our lives. They want to tear us apart: mind, body and soul. But we can take heart, because Jesus is always stronger than the devil and his demons.

Reflect and respond

1. *How does it make you feel to know that spiritually you are just as lost as the man in this passage?*
2. *How has meeting Jesus changed you?*
3. *How has today's devotions challenged you to think differently about the spiritual realm?*

Restoring God,
Thank you that no one's brokenness is ever too hard for you to heal.
Thank you that you draw near to the lonely and the broken-hearted.
Thank you that you never give up on anyone, even when the rest of the world does.
Thank you for your mercy and tenderness.
You are so kind.
Help me to see how much I need your free gift of restoration.
I want to experience more of you today: more of your presence, your grace, and your joy.
Restore me, and heal me.
And teach me how to draw near to others who are hurting, so that I can bring your healing into their lives too.

In Jesus name,
Amen

Meditation verse for the day:

The Lord is close to the brokenhearted;
and saves those who are crushed in spirit...
The Lord will rescue his servants;
no one who takes refuge in him
will be condemned.
(Psalm 34:18, 22)

Day 16

The Sick Woman

(Read Mark 5:21–34)

In today's passage, Jesus heals another sick person. We read so many stories of miraculous healings in the Gospels that it can be easy to start skimming over them, but each one has been deliberately written down to show us more of who God is. So let's not rush through this story and miss the incredible things God's revealing to us about himself through this particular healing.

The bleeding woman

The woman who is healed in verse 29 has been bleeding from her vagina for twelve years. Even in modern times, this would be a horrible problem to have. But understanding the cultural context here will help us to see just how deep this woman's suffering was. Under Jewish religious law, a woman with her period was ceremonially unclean, and she was not allowed to participate in any religious activities in the temple until her bleeding stopped. So for twelve long years, this woman had not been welcome at any of the celebrations and festivals that were central to community life for her people. She would have felt lonely and isolated. Other people probably wouldn't get too close to her because touching her would make them ceremonially unclean as well. She may not have been able to have children because of her medical problem, and it's likely that no one would have wanted to marry her. Even if she was married, her husband would not be allowed to touch her. In a culture where a woman's main value came from being a wife and mother, this would have been devastating. Verse 26 tells us that she had given all her money to doctors who only made her condition worse. Who knows what painful treatments she had to face as those doctors tried to help her. This is a woman who has tried everything, and has lost all hope.

Approaching Jesus

This woman doesn't ask Jesus for healing the way other people do. She's too ashamed and scared to stand up in front of the crowd and say what she needs out loud. She feels too unworthy of having his attention on her. She even seems a little superstitious in how she approaches Jesus, hoping to secretly touch his robe and be healed, as if his clothing is somehow magical. She doesn't approach him in a way that's theologically correct, or in a way we would think should work.

We might expect Jesus to respond angrily here. As a religious leader, he has every right to be upset if a ceremonially unclean person touches him. As Holy God, he has every right to demand that we approach him in a way that shows the utmost respect and honor. He could have rejected her for being so bold or superstitious. He could have told her she needed to ask properly before he would help her. That's obviously what she expected too—just look at the way she shakes in fear in verse 33!

But Jesus is less worried about doing things the 'right' way, and more concerned that she's hurting and needs his help. I absolutely love the gentle response Jesus has for this lonely, shame-filled woman. He says to her, "Daughter, your faith has healed you. Go in peace and be freed from your suffering." What a gracious, merciful Savior we have! He tenderly calls her daughter, and blesses her with peace and freedom. His language is so encouraging, reassuring her in front of the whole crowd that he cares for her. He doesn't tell her off for approaching him in the wrong way. He sees her, and honors her, and gladly sets her free.

Sometimes we worry about how to approach God. We might have been taught that we have to pray certain words for God to forgive us. We might feel like we don't know the Bible well enough for God to listen to us. We might be ashamed of how unworthy we are, and feel the urge to fix up our lives a bit before we try and talk to God. We panic that he'll turn us away because we aren't doing it exactly right.

The Sick Woman

This woman's powerful testimony shows us that our Father welcomes us to him, just as we are. We don't have to know all the right things to think or say or do. We don't have to let our shame and our problems keep us away from him. In fact, our pain is exactly what he wants us to bring to him. Jesus says, in one of the most encouraging and beautiful promises in the Bible: "Come to me, all you who are weary and burdened, and I will give you rest" (Matthew 11:28). See, what really matters isn't how we come, but *who we're coming to*. It's not about how messy our life is, but that we bring all the mess to him. We aren't saved because we're worthy, but because our God loves to give undeserved grace to the unworthy. We aren't loved by God because we are loveable, but because he is Love.

Jesus is saying to you today, "Are you in pain? Full of shame? Exhausted from trying to do it on your own? Come to me. Let me carry the weight of it all for you. Let me love you." All that matters is that we're humble enough to know we need him. So run to him, just the way you are, right now. Don't hold anything back. Use whatever words you have. Trust that he's the only one who can save you. He's waiting for you with eyes filled with love, and a voice filled with compassion. And in his presence you'll find healing, and freedom, and peace. He is such a kind Father.

Reflect and respond

1. *What's something from today's passage that you're thankful for?*
2. *What's something from today's passage that challenges you, and why?*

Loving Father,
Thank you that you love me more than I could ever imagine.
Thank you that while I was still your enemy, you gave your only Son for me.
I worship you for your loving kindness and your mercy, which I don't deserve at all.
Thank you that you welcome me as I am, and offer to change me from the inside out.
Help me come to you with humble boldness, confident in your faithfulness.
Holy Spirit, teach me to understand how deep and wide and high and long the love of God is for me.

In Jesus name,
Amen

Meditation verse for the day:

Come to me,
all you who are weary and burdened,
and I will give you rest.
(Matthew 11:28)

Day 17

The Dead Girl

(READ MARK 5:21-43)

Trusting God's timing

OUR PASSAGE TODAY STARTS with a synagogue leader called Jairus falling on the ground in front of Jesus, begging him to save his sick little girl. Jairus is a powerful, well-respected man in the local community, so for him to publicly humble himself by kneeling in the dirt before Jesus is a huge deal. He's acknowledging in front of the crowd that he desperately needs help. He knows that Jesus is his only hope. He's willing to throw away his pride for the sake of his daughter's life. All the way through the Bible, we see over and over and over again that God loves to bless humble people. He loves to answer people who ask him for help. He loves to rescue people who know how much they need him.

Jesus is on his way to Jairus' house to heal his little girl, when he stops to interact with the bleeding woman whose story we read yesterday. Can you imagine how Jairus felt in that moment? His beloved little girl is in need of *urgent* help, and Jesus focuses on healing a woman who's already been sick for twelve long years. Surely she can wait an extra hour to be healed, right? Did Jesus get his priorities wrong here? Jairus was probably frantic, doubting Jesus' wisdom, desperate for Jesus to hurry, wondering if he'd been right to trust Jesus in the first place. And then the terrible news comes in verse 35: Jesus is too late. Jairus' daughter has died.

We all have times in life where it feels like God has missed the chance to help us. We feel like he's too slow. We wonder where he is, or why he's forgotten about us. We blame him for not helping us with what we think we need, when we think we needed it. We know that Jairus' story has a happy ending, but in our own lives it's usually not so simple. So how do we learn to trust God's timing?

The Bible has so many amazingly encouraging things to say about this. For example, 2 Peter 3:8 tells us that God is never late, and reminds us that God's perspective on time is completely different to ours. We can't ever accuse him of being late when we don't understand the full picture the way that he does. God alone sees how every single event and action in each human's life will impact every other event through the whole of history. He sees the billions of tiny ripple effects that we will never know about. Only he knows what we really need and when we really need it. Only he knows the end of our story—not just for us, but also for our children and grandchildren and great-grandchildren. Our challenge is to trust that *he* is God, and to be humble enough to know that we are not.

We need to preach this truth to our scared hearts when we're starting to lose hope. We need to stand in reverence and humility before this God of ours who's outside of time, and remind ourselves that he promises to always give us what we need right when we need it. Not before we need it. And never too late. God is always on time. Wait patiently for him, trusting that he always knows exactly what he's doing.

"Don't be afraid; just believe."

In verse 36 Jesus speaks some very simple words to Jairus in the darkest moment of his life: "Don't be afraid; just believe." Throughout the Bible, God tells his children not to fear hundreds and hundreds of times, especially when they're in particularly dangerous or scary situations. It seems like God is really eager to give us the gift of fearlessness! And yet so many of us live lives saturated with fear. We get anxious about all the things we can't control. We stress about things that happened in the past and things that might happen in the future. We're terrified of losing the people and things we love most. We even obsessively worry about things happening on the other side of the world that have absolutely nothing to do with us. Jesus' encouraging words are for us today too: *"Don't be afraid; just believe."*

But how do we know what to believe? People have so many different ideas about God, so how can we know what's actually true about him? Thankfully, God gives us the Bible to teach us about himself. He doesn't expect us to guess or make anything up ourselves. He explains who he is in permanent, written, human words that we can understand, and invites us to read and get to know him. He kindly gives us the Holy Spirit to help us make sense of what the Bible says. He also gives us the life of Jesus to show us who he is. Jesus is the fullness of God in a human body, living out his God-ness in ways we can see and hear and understand.

So Jesus is saying to all of us here, "Believe in me. Follow me and get to know me properly. Don't believe everything you hear about me: Listen to my words for yourself. Trust that I am who I say I am. Rest in me. Stake your life on me. Get to know my promises, and believe that I always keep them. Have faith in me. And when you believe in me—*really* believe—you won't have to fear anything." Do you believe him?

Reflect and respond

1. *When have you struggled to trust God's timing?*
2. *What are your deepest fears? When do you struggle with anxiety in daily life?*
3. *In the darkest moments of your life, how can you guard your heart against fear?*

Everlasting God,
I repent of my pride.
Forgive me for assuming that I know what's best for my own life.
Forgive me for not trusting your timing.
Please teach me more about who you are, so that I can trust you more.
Help me believe in your promises, so that I can have a peace that passes understanding.
Please free me from the fear that's threatening to drown me.
Give me faith.
I want to rest in you, safe and secure and fearless.

In Jesus name,
Amen

Meditation verse for the day:

So do not fear, for I am with you;
do not be dismayed, for I am your God.
I will strengthen you and help you;
I will uphold you
with my righteous right hand.
(Isaiah 41:10)

Day 18

Fishing for People

(Read Mark 6:1–29)

The familiar Jesus

Today we read about Jesus going to teach in his hometown, and being rejected by the people he grew up with. He teaches in the local synagogue and they're amazed by what they hear, but they're also confused because they can't understand where he got such authority and wisdom from. They're too familiar with him to believe that he is the Messiah, even though he's doing miracles right in front of them. They just can't believe their own eyes: "Who does he think he is? He's just a local guy! His mother lives right down the road, and we know all his brothers and sisters; he's an ordinary guy from an ordinary family. Why does he think he's something special!"

Sometimes Jesus can get too familiar to us as well. We've heard all the stories about him a hundred times, but they don't stir our hearts anymore. We might admire his lifestyle and respect his teachings, but we don't fall down before him in awe and worship anymore. We're a bit bored of him, so we aren't eager to spend time with him any chance we get. Maybe we even get offended by him when he says he's the only way to God. Who does this guy think he is? Sure, he's a nice person, but is he really the Savior of the whole world?

If that's you today, be very careful: Jesus doesn't come where he isn't wanted. He wants to have authority in your life, but he isn't going to take it by force. He loves you, but he won't ever make you love him back. So don't think that just because you go to church on Sundays and know lots about Jesus, that he is your Lord. Don't think because you grew up in a Christian family, that you're saved. Like Jesus' old neighbors and family friends, don't get so comfortable with him that you forget who he really is. Take a few moments now to stop reading and ask yourself the most important questions in life: Am I really a disciple of Jesus? Am I depending completely on Jesus to save me, not trying to save myself? Am I giving him the authority in my life that he deserves? Am I actually trusting and obeying his words?

Jesus sends out the disciples

In verse 7 Jesus sends out his twelve closest followers to share his message. Pay attention to what Jesus tells his disciples in verses 8 and 9: They're packing light for this mission. They don't need to stock up on anything before they go. Jesus is making sure they aren't going to depend on their own money or their own food or their own resources to help them be successful. He wants them to depend on God alone. He wants them to trust him for everything they'll need for each new day. Jesus is the one who's been teaching them everything they need to know. He's the one who gives them spiritual authority over evil spirits. Everything they need will come from him.

There's a popular saying: God will never give you more than you can handle. That's not true. It's not anywhere in the Bible. In fact, the Bible tells us the exact opposite! God will *definitely* give us more than we can handle on our own! Why? So that we have to depend on him to be everything we need, and can experience for ourselves just how trustworthy he is. It's a scenario that we see over and over again in the Bible. God always chooses scared people, weak people, unskilled people, marginalized people, and young people, to do important work for him. And his promise to them is always the same: "Don't be afraid, I will be with you. Just do what I tell you to do and trust me for the rest."

Fishing for people

Look again at the very start of verse 14. It tells us that Jesus' disciples are making such a huge impact that even King Herod hears about them. They're driving out demons and healing sick people. They're preaching with authority. They left home without even a spare shirt, and now they're transforming lives up and down the countryside to the point that even King Herod is wondering what's going on! What an encouraging testimony of what Jesus can do through us when we humbly offer our lives up to him. We bring him the few small skills we have, and God loves to use us for his glory.

But this passage also reminds us that we won't always have earthly success in our mission. Just because we're in the right place doing the right work for God in God's own power, doesn't mean it will always be easy or have the results we're hoping for. Jesus warns his disciples that some people will reject their message, just like they rejected Jesus himself in his own hometown. In fact, it could get much worse than that. John the Baptist had his head chopped off. Jesus was crucified. Most of the twelve disciples eventually ended up getting killed for spreading Jesus' message. Even today Christians are being arrested or killed all around the world as they courageously share their faith with the people around them. I love this quote from Mother Teresa, when she was asked why she spent her whole life caring for poor people who were about to die anyway: "God has not called me to be successful . . . God has called me to be faithful."[1] All the people Mother Teresa served died. Every single one. She kept serving them anyway. She just focused on obeying God, year after year, decade after decade, and trusted the results to him.

Reflect and respond

1. *Do you regularly see fresh glimpses of Jesus' majesty in the Bible, or has he become too familiar to inspire much awe in your heart?*

2. *What do you depend on to get you through each day? What do you feel like you can't go without, especially in hard times?*

3. *How can you practice relying on Jesus to be everything you need?*

---

1. Spink, *Mother Teresa*, 245.

Oh Lord,
I really want to be your disciple, but sometimes it's pretty scary.
I want to follow you, but I don't want you to ask me to do hard things.
I like being comfortable and safe, and I enjoy being respected by people.
Please give me courage to share your love with the people around me.
Help me trust your wonderful promises to me, so that I can boldly follow you no matter where you lead.
Show me that you're everything I need.
Use my life for your glory!

In Jesus name,
Amen

Meditation verse for the day:

We were crushed and overwhelmed
beyond our ability to endure,
and we thought we would never live through it.
In fact, we expected to die.
But as a result, we stopped relying on ourselves
and learned to rely only on God, who raises the dead.
(2 Corinthians 1:8–9, NLT)

Day 19

Rest and Miracles

(Read Mark 6:30–56)

Making time for rest

I just love the helpful advice Jesus gives his apostles in verse 31. They've been so busy doing the important work of serving and healing and teaching the people around them, that they haven't had a chance to eat for a while. Jesus invites them to get away with him to a quiet place where they can rest together. Most of us live very busy lives. Many modern cultures encourage us to work hard and play hard, racing through life until we burn out or break down. Our self-worth is often wrapped up in how productive we are, and regular rest can be looked down on as laziness or wasted time.

As Christians we often focus on our spiritual wellbeing, but Jesus wisely recognizes that his disciples have other needs as well. They need to eat well and rest well and enjoy downtime with close friends to be healthy and whole human beings. God made our bodies, and he cares about them. Looking after our physical bodies and our emotional wellbeing is a way to honor God with the life he's given us. Taking the time to rest also helps us remember that we aren't the saviors of the world. No matter how busy you are—even if you're busy doing God's work—prioritize time to rest well. Build downtime into your schedule. Eat nourishing food. Move your body. Regularly spend time with Christian friends. Go to therapy. Look after yourself spiritually, emotionally, and physically.

Authority

Today's passage covers two of Jesus' most famous miracles: feeding thousands of people with a few small loaves and fish; and walking on water. Once again, let's not rush through because we might already be familiar with these stories. Instead, take a moment now to pray that God will amaze you with something new and beautiful about himself today.

The most obvious message of these two miracles is that Jesus is like no other human in the history of the world. No one else has ever been able to multiply five loaves of bread and two fish into enough food to feed thousands and thousands of people. No one else on earth has ever been able to walk on water. Even with all our amazing technology in modern times, no one can do these things. Jesus has incredible authority over the natural world. It makes sense, doesn't it? After all, he is its Creator. Hebrews 1:2–3 tells us that God created the whole universe through Jesus, and that Jesus keeps everything going through his power. It all exists because of him. No wonder he's completely sovereign, powerfully in control of it all.

The authority of Jesus is a strong theme we've seen all the way through Mark's Gospel. We've read about Jesus showing his authority over evil spirits, sickness, disabilities, nature, and even death. He teaches with an authority that amazes everyone who hears him. We've read that he has authority to forgive sins, and authority over the Sabbath. But what about Jesus' authority over you? Did you know that the apostle Peter calls Jesus our Master? Or that Paul says God bought us with a price, so our lives don't belong to us anymore? How does that make you feel? We don't like the idea of having a master. It's in our nature to resist authority. We hesitate to surrender ourselves fully to God because we like the feeling of being in charge of our own lives.

We want to define our own identity.
We want to decide how to spend our time and money.
We want to use our bodies any way we like.
We want to trust our own feelings to tell us what is right and wrong.
We want to decide what truth is for ourselves.

If you're still uncomfortable with the idea of giving Jesus all authority in your life, today's passage has great encouragement for you. Look again at verses 42 and 43. What does Jesus do with his power and authority in this story? He cares for people. He loves them and looks after them. They're hungry and he feeds them. And he doesn't just give them a bit of food. He makes sure they all eat until they're *completely satisfied*. He fills them right up. And he provides so extravagantly for them that there are still twelve whole baskets full of food left over! Now look at Jesus walking on the water in verse 51. He doesn't just calm the wind, he climbs right into the boat with the disciples. He draws near to them when they are terrified and sits with them and comforts them. He gives them the gift of his own presence to encourage and love them when they need it most.

God wants you to surrender your whole life to him, which goes against our nature. But don't be afraid. He's a compassionate Master who shows abundant generosity to his people. He's a kind King who invites us to feast at his banquet table and share in his joy. He's a humble God who kneels on the floor and washes our dirty, tired feet. He's the Good Shepherd who lays down his life for his sheep, gently guiding us to lush green pastures and encouraging us to lie down and rest there, while he restores our souls. The idea that Jesus should have all authority over you might feel oppressive in our culture of radical independence. But he doesn't want to burden you. He bought you at a great cost to himself, so that he could set you free from being a slave to sin. Jesus has every right to our lives. But he uses his authority for our good. Do you trust him?

Reflect and respond

1. *How are you looking after yourself spiritually, emotionally, and physically, as a way of honoring the life God gave you? How could you be doing this better?*
2. *How does it make you feel to think about submitting every part of your life and self under God's authority? Why does it make you feel that way?*
3. *How has this passage encouraged you to trust God as your King?*

Almighty God,
You are my Creator.
You have all authority in the heavens and on earth.
Who am I, that you love me?
Who am I, that you call me your child?
I can never thank you enough, my Lord and my God.
Please search my heart and help me see the areas of my life that I haven't surrendered to you yet.
Please forgive me for trying to do life my own way.
Help me let go of my need to control everything.
Help me to believe that you're completely worthy of my trust.
I want to taste and see your goodness.

In Jesus name,
Amen

Meditation verse for the day:

He tends his flock like a shepherd:
He gathers the lambs in his arms
and carries them close to his heart;
he gently leads those that have young.
(Isaiah 40:11)

Day 20

The Heart of a Pharisee

(READ MARK 7:1-23)

ALL THROUGH THE GOSPELS Jesus saves his harshest language for the Pharisees. It's really easy to see them as the bad guys in the story. Be careful judging them, though! We are usually much more like the Pharisees than we want to admit. So stop right now and pray. Ask the Holy Spirit to give you the humility to see the Pharisee inside yourself.

No love for God

The Pharisees and teachers of the law do really well at being good. They're very moral people. They're religious professionals! But Jesus can see into their hearts, and he knows they're not motivated by love for God. He says in verse 6: "These people honor me with their lips, but their hearts are far from me." That means they're saying and doing all the right things, but not for the right reason. They're hypocrites, because who they are on the outside doesn't match who they are on the inside. Jesus is warning us here that God isn't honored by people who do good stuff but don't actually love him. We can be the nicest, best, holiest person in the whole world, but God isn't pleased with any of it if we're motivated by fear or selfishness or tradition. You see, God's deepest desire is to be in a loving relationship with you. He longs for you to adore him as much as he adores you. He wants your whole heart, not just good behavior.

Does verse 6 also describe you? Do you honor God with your lips without actually loving him in your heart? If you're feeling uncomfortable here, don't rush through this. It's actually a life or death question. You see, the scariest thing is that the Pharisees here show us that someone can be perfectly religious and still be lost in God's eyes. You can be a respected, powerful spiritual leader and be spiritually dead without realizing it. That's why it's so important to reflect deeply and honestly here. So maybe you go to church every Sunday, and memorize Bible verses, and do your devotions every day, and never use curse words... but why? Do you do it all so you don't get into trouble with your parents? Do you do it because it makes you feel good to be a good person? Because you want other people to think you're nice? Because you're scared of going to hell? Because you grew up in a Christian-y culture? Or do you do it because you love God and genuinely want to honor him?

Self righteousness

In verses 8 and 9 Jesus also accuses the religious leaders of making up their own rules for righteousness instead of following God's commands. They make up lists of what to do and what not to do, patting themselves on the back for being better than other people. This is called *self-righteousness*, which means trying to earn God's approval by acting right and believing the right stuff. Self-righteous people believe that being saved is all about doing the right things. Because remember, the Pharisees aren't bad guys, they're just passionate Jewish nationalists who are trying to protect their way of life and values from outsiders. Remind you of anyone? It's easy to point fingers, but take a good, hard look inside yourself. We all regularly slip into self-righteousness, because it's easier to change our behavior than to surrender our whole lives to Jesus. We all like to look down on other people, telling ourselves that we've got it right and they've got it wrong. We judge others for their choices and beliefs, and we think that they aren't proper Christians like we are. We use traditions from our culture or our church to measure holiness, instead of listening to God's own voice. Here the Pharisees are being judgmental over hand-washing traditions, but these days it might sound more like this: Real Christians don't vote that way. Real Christians aren't friends with LGBTQ+ people. Real Christians don't dress that way or date that way or listen to that kind of music. Real Christians don't drink alcohol. Real Christian women have lots of babies and stay in the home. As hard as it is to hear, putting our religious traditions above the word of God is a huge problem in the Western church. But God doesn't want us doing things for the sake of tradition. What he cares about is how faithfully we love him, and how faithfully we love our neighbors.

What comes out of our hearts

In verses 21 and 22, Jesus explains things in more detail to his disciples, who are a bit confused by it all. (By the way, if you often struggle to understand what Jesus means, don't stress! You aren't alone. The disciples regularly needed help understanding him, and so do the rest of us.) Jesus explains that the religious leaders are focused on the wrong things. Our unrighteousness—which means our spiritual uncleanness before God—comes from what's *inside* us, not from our behavior. We're not separated from God by how dirty our hands are or because we sometimes swear, or because we didn't dress modestly enough for church. We're separated from our perfectly holy God by the sin deep in our hearts. Jesus has been the only perfect human in existence. All the rest of us are spiritually dirty before God. The religious leaders thought they could make themselves clean by doing complicated washing rituals. Jesus tells us here that sin is much too deeply ingrained in our hearts for washing to help. The sinful things that bubble up from inside us can't just be washed away. It can be easy to skim the list of sins here and assume they don't really apply to us. Many of us will never steal or murder or commit adultery, for example. But look closer. Greed? Envy? Slander? Pride? I don't know about you, but I personally struggle with most of those every single day. I want more nice stuff, and am envious of people whose lives seem better than mine. I'm tempted to gossip about people. I judge other people because I feel like I'm better than them in some way. This list of heart-sins applies to every single one of us.

But thankfully, the gospel promises us something much better than the Pharisees' washing rituals. When we put our faith in him, Jesus washes us clean with his blood once and for all. On the cross he took our eternal punishment on himself and wiped our record clean forever. God no longer sees any of those sins when he looks at us, because they've already been completely paid for! The Bible calls this *justification*, which means that our guilt is taken away forever, and Jesus makes us perfectly right with God. The beautiful news of the gospel is that Jesus has already done everything needed to save us. This free gift is grace. It isn't something we could ever deserve. All we have to do is be humble enough to receive it. When we try to earn salvation by our good behavior, we tragically miss the whole story of grace. We spend our lives working harder and harder, following more and more rules, always worrying that we aren't good enough and feeling horribly guilty every time we mess up. Grace frees us from all of that. Grace brings freedom, because we know our salvation isn't up to us. We didn't earn it, so we can't lose it.

Reflect and respond

1. *How do you sometimes try to earn God's approval?*
2. *What behaviors do you think makes someone a good Christian? What behaviors do you judge other Christians for? Are these behaviors from culture or from the Bible?*
3. *What sins in your heart is God leading you to repent for today?*

Oh God,
Be merciful to me, because I'm a sinner!
I repent for the deeply rooted sins that are inside me. Please forgive me.
Thank you that my sin doesn't have power over me anymore—I belong to you!
Thank you for forgiving me.
Thank you for saving me.
Thank you for your free grace!
Holy Spirit, please do your holy work deep in my heart and soul and mind.
Change me from the inside.
Make me more like Jesus.

In Jesus name,
Amen

Meditation verse for the day:

For everyone has sinned;
we all fall short of God's glorious standard.
Yet God, in his grace, freely makes us right in his sight.
He did this through Christ Jesus
when he freed us from the penalty for our sins.
(Romans 3:23–24, NLT)

Day 21

The Gentile Woman

(READ MARK 7:24–30)

JESUS WANTS TO FIND some peace and quiet, so he heads off to the area around Tyre, which is now modern-day Lebanon. This region is filled with people the Bible calls *Gentiles*, which means that they aren't ethnically Jewish. They have different religious and cultural practices. In fact, the woman who begs Jesus for help in this passage is from a people group that had historically been bitter enemies of the Jews.

This woman comes to Jesus in complete desperation and humility. In verses 25 and 26 we see that she falls down at Jesus' feet and begs him to heal her little girl. In the parallel version of this story in Matthew 15:22, she cries out "Lord, Son of David, have mercy on me!" Even though she's not Jewish, she calls Jesus these particular names to show him that she knows who he is and believes in his authority to save her precious daughter. In response, Jesus says words that might sound really rude to us at first glance: "First let the children eat all they want, for it is not right to take the children's bread and toss it to the dogs" (verse 27). When he talks about the children, he is meaning the Jews, and when he mentions the dogs, he is talking about the Gentiles/all non-Jewish people. The bread in the metaphor is the message of salvation he brings to the world.

Jesus speaks in parables

Jesus is speaking in parables again. He's using a picture to explain that the first focus of his ministry on earth is the Jewish people, who are the descendants of the Israelites, God's original chosen people. Jesus specifically uses the word "first" here, so he's definitely not saying that God's salvation is *only* for Jewish people. This means that God is also going to invite Gentiles into his family, but that mission will come next. In Matthew 28:19 we read that Jesus' last instructions to his disciples were to "go and make disciples of all nations," and all of the biblical prophesies about heaven describe it being gloriously filled with diverse people from all cultures and tribes and languages! So, we know that Jesus is definitely not being racist toward this woman. The kingdom of heaven is not only for one group of people. Jesus doesn't only care about Jewish people, and he definitely isn't rudely rejecting everyone else. He lovingly sacrificed his life to save people from every single people group on earth!

So, if Jesus isn't being rude here, why is he talking like this? Let's remember that he's using a parable. In Matthew 13:10 the disciples ask Jesus why he speaks in parables so much, and he answers that it's so not everyone will be able to understand him. It's like a riddle. They'll hear his words, but because their hearts are hard towards God, the words will mean nothing to them. Jesus speaks in parables to test who's *really* interested in finding the truth, and who's humble enough to listen carefully to the Holy Spirit with open ears and eyes and hearts.

The stunning thing in this story is that the Gentile woman understands the parable immediately! She isn't offended or confused by Jesus' words, and she even answers him using his own metaphor. In verse 28 she is confidently saying to him: "I know I'm not worthy, but I also know that even the tiniest crumb from you will be more than enough for me." She shows a humble boldness in the way she perseveres in asking for her daughter's healing. Jesus is impressed by her deep wisdom and faith. This woman clearly has the spiritual eyes to see and ears to hear the truth about who Jesus is. Don't forget that half the time Jesus' own disciples don't even understand his parables, and need to ask him to explain them! I just love how encouraging this is for every one of us. There isn't a single person on earth who isn't welcome into the kingdom of God. It doesn't matter what our background is, or how much we know about God. The Holy Spirit can open up anyone's eyes to see Jesus for who he really is.

The Gentile Woman

Jesus and women

Some modern people accuse the Bible of discriminating against woman, so it's really important to take this opportunity to look more closely at how Jesus behaves here. Kenneth Bailey, an expert in understanding the culture Jesus lived in, says that Jesus treated women in a radically different way than the other Jewish rabbis around him. He explains that when this Gentile woman begged Jesus for help, it would have been culturally appropriate for Jesus to completely ignore her! Jesus' own disciples might have expected him to just turn his head away and pretend he didn't even see her. Bailey says, "A self-respecting rabbi did not even talk to his wife in a public place."[1] In a culture where rabbis weren't meant to speak to their own female family members outside the home, can you even imagine what it meant for Jesus to talk publicly with this non-Jewish woman? And he not only speaks to her, but he openly admires her wisdom, and honors her request! Jesus is smashing through deeply ingrained gender and ethnic boundaries here. He's challenging the prejudiced attitudes of his society, demonstrating his compassionate love for *all* people, everywhere, with no exceptions. He's setting an example for his disciples, and for all of us who belong to his kingdom, regardless of what the culture around us says.

Reflect and respond

1. *Reflect on the fact that heaven will be filled with people from every people group. How does that influence your life as a Christian here on earth?*

2. *What prejudices does your particular culture/family hold against certain groups of people? How can you show the wide-open love of Jesus to the people your community treats as being less worthy?*

3. *How can the humble boldness of this woman encourage or inspire you when you pray?*

---

1. Bailey, *Middle Eastern Eyes*, 212.

Loving God,
I can't wait for heaven.
I can't wait to stand before your throne with all your children from every nation, tribe, and people. I can't wait to worship you with my spiritual brothers and sisters, singing to you in every language.
Thank you that your salvation is for all people, everywhere.
I long for your kingdom to come on earth as it is in heaven.
Search my heart and show me the patterns of judgment and discrimination that my culture or my family have taught me.
Give me a clean heart, Holy Spirit.
Help me change how I think about groups of people that I look down on.
Help me love without boundaries, like Jesus.
Help me to love others in ways that show people what life in your kingdom is like.

In Jesus name,
Amen

Meditation verse for the day:

In Christ's family there can be no division
into Jew and non-Jew, slave and free,
male and female. Among us you are all equal.
(Galatians 3:28, MSG)

Day 22

The Deaf Man

(Read Mark 7:31-37)

The kindness of Jesus

Today's passage is full to the brim of God's extravagant loving-kindness. Jesus is still wandering around in Gentile (non-Jewish) lands, being followed around by a crowd. As usual, people are asking him for healing, and Mark focuses in on the healing of one man in particular. This man had to be brought to Jesus by others. He couldn't hear anything and could hardly talk, so he might have struggled to ask Jesus to heal him on his own. If we're honest, many of us feel uncomfortable around people living with severe disabilities, and aren't sure where to look or what to say. But Jesus doesn't hesitate or feel awkward. He leads the man to a private spot, away from the distractions of the crowd. And then he puts his fingers in the man's ears, and touches his tongue. We know that Jesus is able to heal people without being physically near them, so why does he touch this man in such a specific way? And why does Mark—who famously doesn't include a lot of detail in his writing—include so much specific information about this particular healing?

Pastor Sinclair Ferguson explains: "The man could not hear Jesus and he was also incapable of verbal communication. So Jesus 'spoke' to him in the language he could understand—sign-language."[1] Read that over again slowly, and let it just break your heart wide open in thankfulness to Jesus. What a caring Savior he is! Jesus has so much compassion for this Gentile man, and he meets him right where he is. He gives him his full attention, leaving behind the crowds to focus on one hurting individual. He communicates to him in a thoughtful and careful way. He touches the man's damaged ears, and his struggling tongue, to show that he understands. He tailors his approach to this man's unique situation, making sure that he feels comfortable and safe and involved. Jesus' gentle touch tells this man, "I see you. I am for you. I will help you."

Verse 34 tells us that before healing the man, Jesus looks up to heaven and gives a deep sigh. Once again, Jesus is communicating to the man in a visual way that he can understand with his disability. By looking upwards, he's showing that it's God's power that will heal this man. He wants the man to give glory to God alone. His big sigh is important too. The man can see Jesus' empathy through his body language. Ferguson says this sigh is "an expression of the deep sorrow and anger our Lord felt at the ravages of the Fall in the lives of men. The sigh was the sigh of the heart of God for his needy creation."[2] Jesus is using his body language to show his heartbreak at the suffering this man has experienced. He's communicating his sadness and anger over the brokenness that's in this world because of sin. This is the grief-filled sigh of a personal God who cares about every tear his children have ever cried. Jesus wants this man to know that he's not just going to help him, but also that he deeply loves him. What a wonderful, kind God we have.

Let Jesus love you

Satan loves to lie to us, telling us that our brokenness separates us from Jesus. He loves to make us feel ashamed of our secret sins, or isolated in our suffering, so that we hide our pain away under a fake smile. He loves to make us feel like we're too broken for Jesus to actually love us, or be able to heal us. But those are lies from the pit of hell. Satan's goal is to keep us away from the kindness and freedom that Jesus wants to give us. He tries to complicate the story, convincing us we need to fix ourselves up a bit before Jesus will really love us.

1. Ferguson, *Mark*, 114.
2. Ferguson, *Mark*, 115.

The Deaf Man

But Jesus never says that. Instead, he makes it super simple. In a verse we've already read a few times before (because it's just *that* good), Jesus says there is only one step needed: "Come to me, all you who are weary and burdened, and I will give you rest." So in Jesus' own words, how do we get to experience his love? All we have to do is come to him. That's it. Just come. Open ourselves up to him. Turn to him. Let him in. Receive his love. In fact, that suffering and loneliness and shame and hurt that we think separates us from God? That's exactly the stuff Jesus is saying to bring with us when we come. He's waiting to exchange our mess for his rest. And if you're worried your mess will be too much for him, here's another promise from the mouth of Jesus himself: "Whoever comes to me I will never drive away" (John 6:37). You don't need to fear being rejected by Jesus. There's zero chance he'll change his mind about you at the last moment. Just come to him. Pastor Dane Ortlund captures it beautifully:

> "He intends to restore you into the radiant resplendence for which you were created. And that is dependant not on you keeping yourself clean but on you taking your mess to him. . . His power runs so deep that he is able to redeem the very worst parts of our past into the most radiant parts of our future. But we need to take those dark miseries to him."[3]

Restoration to radiant resplendence, that's what Jesus has planned for you! That means shining magnificence! Dazzling glory! Stunning brilliance! Beautiful splendor! There's nothing average or ordinary happening here. He has a unique healing ready for you, exactly tailored for your unique pain. What are you waiting for?!

Reflect and respond

1. *What deep shame or hurt feels like it's keeping you from Jesus? What makes you think, "Oh, Jesus couldn't possibly want to be close to me because of that."*

2. *Have you come to Jesus with your heavy burdens, or is something stopping you from really believing in his love for you? (If this is a very hard or emotional question for you, please find a trusted Christian mentor or therapist who can help you work through it.)*

---

3. Ortlund, *Gentle and Lowly*, 160–161.

Merciful God,
You're so kind.
Thank you for the way you tenderly care for me, in exactly the ways I need most.
Thank you for meeting me right where I am, in all my weakness and brokenness.
Your heart breaks at my pain.
You're angry at the damage sin has done in my life.
You're waiting with open arms for me to come to you with all my mess.
You're excited to make something radiantly beautiful out of my life.
Help me believe that all of this really is true.
Help me come to you, so that I can lay my burdens down and receive the gift of your rest.
I love you.

In Jesus name,
Amen

Meditation verse for the day:

I pray that you will be able to understand
how wide and how long and how high
and how deep his love is.
(Ephesians 3:18, NLV)

Day 23

Feeding Thousands

(READ MARK 8:1–21)

A little in the hands of Jesus

JESUS IS ONCE AGAIN surrounded by a huge crowd of hungry people, and he feels compassion on them. He's already spent three days with them by this stage, teaching them and healing people, but he also cares deeply about their most basic physical needs. I just love what Jesus does here by asking the disciples how much food they've got with them. This is the Lord of all creation we're talking about here. He spoke and galaxies popped into existence! He definitely could have made food suddenly appear out of nowhere if he wanted to. But instead, Jesus invites the disciples to participate in his miracle. He asks for their help, and lets them contribute the small amount they have. He provides abundantly for thousands of people out of the simple lunches they offer to him.

This is also the way God chooses to build his kingdom. Our God has all power and authority on heaven and earth. He could bring salvation to the ends of the earth without involving a single human being. He could send his angels, or reveal himself to people in dreams and visions. In fact, in just the first two chapters of the Gospel of Matthew, God uses angels and dreams to communicate to people five different times! He still does show himself to people all around the world today in supernatural ways like that, but God's more common way of spreading his message is to use normal

Christians just like us. He calls *us* to go out into all the world and make disciples of all nations. It seems like a crazy plan. It seems totally inefficient, and very risky. But it's also breath-takingly kind. God invites us to partner with him in writing the most important story the world has ever known. He uses us to shine his love into the lives of our neighbors and families and friends. He empowers us to be his messengers, carrying his hope and joy all around the world.

And the most wonderful part is this: When we bring our humble lives and lay them at his feet, he always uses us in incredible ways. We set apart our few loaves of bread for him and he makes them into a feast. We obediently follow him along the simple path of faith, and he leads us to wild and beautiful places we could never have imagined for ourselves. He wants to use your life to do something that will make a difference in eternity! Now don't misunderstand me here; I'm not saying you have to burn yourself out doing big things for God. I'm also not saying God will necessarily use your gifts in huge, miraculous ways that will make you a famous spiritual leader. God's mustard-seed kingdom isn't in the business of flashy displays of power. Remember: Greatness in God's eyes often looks very different from what we expect. We're talking about the God who loves to be kind to lonely people and to give hugs to children. He wants to use you to bring his love to others in beautiful and radical ways. He wants to use the little you offer him to bring healing and renewal to the people and communities around you.

A living sacrifice

There's also a challenge hidden in this passage, for each and every one of us. Look at the order of how things happen here. First, Jesus draws the disciples' attention to the needs of the people around them. "Look at all these hungry people who I love!" Then, the disciples are overwhelmed and panic a bit: "Mmm... what does that have to do with us? We're in the middle of nowhere; we can't do anything about it!" So Jesus asks them point blank what food they have, which must have seemed a bit absurd to them in the face of how huge the crowd was. But after they lay down everything they have, Jesus does the miracle and feeds the thousands of hungry people. Reflect on your life right now. Chances are there are some hurting people around you. Some of us are in high-achieving study or work environments where anxiety and loneliness are festering just underneath the surface.

Some of us have friends or family members who are wrestling with depression that threatens to drown them. Some of us live in neighborhoods where homelessness, addiction, and poverty are obvious to see every time we walk down the street. Some of us live in countries where certain groups of people don't have the same opportunities as others. Has God been trying to draw your attention to the particular pain of someone around you? Is there someone you've been praying for, because you're hoping God will save them or heal them? The challenge of this story is that it might just be that God is waiting for *you* to get involved in meeting the needs around you. *You* might be the answer he wants to give to your own prayers. Like the disciples, you might look around and say, "I don't have what it takes to fix all this hurt!" Which is true. You don't, by yourself. But maybe God is asking you, "What do you have to give? Bring it to me, and watch what I can do through you." Look around you. You are there for a reason. Whose brokenness has God put on your heart?

As a young person, you might feel like you don't have much to offer Jesus right now. Our world tends to value experience, and wealth, and success, and influence, and you might not have much of any of those. But Jesus doesn't mind if all you have to give him are some bread rolls or a couple of coins, because the amount you give him isn't what's important. He isn't limited by your limitations. The whole point is that you offer him *everything* you have and *everything* you are, as small as it might seem. Give yourself to him as a living sacrifice, and just watch what his power is able to do! Our God loves to use nobodies. So wherever you are in life, you have something to give him. Your heart. Your time. Your mind. Your money. Your relationships. Your plans for the future. Your study. Your job or career. Your skills. Your passion. Lay it all down before the King's throne, and pray that he will use your life to display the splendor of his majesty. Nothing we offer up to God in love is ever wasted.

Reflect and respond

1. *How does today's devotions encourage you?*
2. *How does today's devotions challenge you?*
3. *What practical steps is the Holy Spirit leading you to take as a result of today's devotions?*

Almighty God,
You are the same powerful God who fed thousands of hungry people from just a handful of food.
Use my little life to bring your hope and love into the hurting places around me.
Put someone on my heart to love in your name today.
I surrender all that I have, and all that I am.
I'm all yours.

In Jesus name,
Amen

Meditation verse for the day:

Therefore, I urge you, brothers and sisters,
in view of God's mercy, to offer your bodies
as a living sacrifice, holy and pleasing to God –
this is your true and proper worship.
(Romans 12:1)

Day 24

The Way of the Cross

(Read Mark 8:22–38)

"Get behind me, Satan!"

IN THIS PASSAGE WE see Peter go from a wonderful spiritual high to a devastating low. In verse 29, he demonstrates that the Holy Spirit is powerfully at work in him, helping him understand glorious spiritual truths. The parallel version of this story in Matthew 16 tells us that Jesus praises and blesses him, promising that Peter will be the rock on which the Christian church would be built. He must have been thrilled! His rabbi has just affirmed him and prophesied that he would become a great spiritual leader! It doesn't get much better than that for a disciple of Jesus.

However, only four verses later, Jesus has to strongly rebuke Peter, angrily saying, "Get behind me, Satan!" What did Peter do to deserve this type of criticism? Once again, the parallel version of the story gives us some helpful extra details. Matthew explains that when Jesus is telling his disciples he would be killed and resurrected, Peter is very upset about it and says to him, "This shall never happen to you" (Matthew 16:22). Peter is trying to convince Jesus that he doesn't need to die. Peter thinks he's supporting Jesus here, but Jesus calls this idea *demonic*! He accuses Peter of thinking in the way of the world, not the way of God. Peter is expecting a Savior who is going to rule in power and glory. But Jesus knows that salvation is only possible through his sacrificial death. There's no other way to complete his mission.

This conversation reminds us that God's ways in building his kingdom are completely opposite to the ways of the world. We like to put our trust in powerful governments, strong militaries, and good laws, but Jesus shows us that his way involves laying down our lives for our enemies. We like to think that if we can just get more political power, or debate people convincingly enough, or grow our online influence, then we can save people and make the world a better place. Jesus says in response: "That way of thinking has no place in my kingdom. Get behind me, Satan!" The way of Jesus is the way of the suffering servant. His way is the slow, quiet way of patient, self-sacrificial, relational, faithful love.

This moment also reminds us that there will never be a time in this life where we don't need to be on guard for Satan's voice in our ear. We'll never be so in-tune with the Holy Spirit that the devil can't quietly sneak in and trick us into believing his lies. And his lies are not usually obvious and nasty! They often look and sound very comfortable and right. The lie Peter believes here is that Jesus can be the Messiah without needing to suffer. That sounds nice. It feels like a *good* plan. But Jesus calls it a lie from Satan! This is why we all need to carefully test everything we believe against what the Bible says, not what feels right and good to us.

The devil is constantly prowling around us like a hungry lion, and often it's when we feel closest to God that he attacks us. Sometimes it's right as God is doing the most wonderful things in our hearts and lives that Satan does his very best to drag us down. It happened to Jesus immediately after his wonderfully powerful baptism experience, when Satan then tempted him in the wilderness. It happened to King David at the height of his success, when he gave in to his lust and destroyed many lives forever. We need to be alert and prepared for a spiritual battle at all times, expecting the devil to attack or to seduce us with his comforting lies. If you aren't sure how to do this, I strongly recommend Priscilla Shirer's fantastic Bible study for teens, called *The Armor of God*.

Denying ourselves

In the final section of this chapter, Jesus says some very challenging words: "Whoever wants to be my disciple must deny themselves and take up their cross and follow me" (verse 34). Jesus is telling us that being his disciple means taking a radically different approach to life than the way the world tells us is best. First he calls us to deny ourselves. This means to stop putting out own desires and feelings first, and to trust God's will for our lives instead. And then he calls us to pick up our cross. This means we need to be prepared to suffer and sacrifice for the sake of Jesus. It means we need to be ok with feeling uncomfortable. We need to expect people to reject us and hate us, and maybe even to kill us because of the God we serve. And lastly he calls us to follow him, surrendering our right to decide how we want to live and following his way instead. I know that none of this sounds like a lot of fun, but Jesus isn't telling us this because he wants us to be miserable. In fact, he says in John 15:11 that his plan for us is the exact opposite: joy, joy and more joy! Fullness of joy! Overflowing joy!

You see, when Jesus calls us to deny ourselves, he wants to save us from ourselves. Right near the start of the Bible in Genesis 3, we read about how sin first came into the world when Adam and Eve put their own desires above what God had told them to do. This is still the root of all sin in the world today. Sin is putting our own desires and feelings and wants and thoughts at the center of our lives. Sin is when we believe that we deserve to be on the throne, not God. We idolize ourselves. Jesus knows that the opposite of idolizing ourselves is denying ourselves. It doesn't mean we hate ourselves (which would be very offensive to God, who made us and adores us.) Self-denial means putting God back on the throne where he rightfully belongs. Self-denial means rejecting our own plans for a good life and trusting God's plan instead. Self-denial means letting God be the main character in our story.

It's counter-intuitive, but Jesus is saying in verses 35 and 36 that the only way to real life is through dying to ourselves. The great philosopher C. S. Lewis once explained it like this:

> "Give up yourself, and you will find your real self. Lose your life and you will save it. Submit to death, death of your ambitions and favourite wishes every day and death of your whole body in the end: submit with every fibre of your being, and you will find eternal life. Keep back nothing... Look for yourself, and you will find in the long run only hatred, loneliness, despair, rage, ruin, and decay. But look for Christ and you will find Him, and with Him everything else thrown in."[1]

Denying ourselves, picking up our cross, and following Jesus is a hard path, and it goes against everything the world tells us is best for us. But Jesus denied himself first, for you. He took up his cross first, for you. And he

---

1. Lewis, *Mere Christianity*, 226–227.

promises that this is the path to true, eternal joy. Do you trust him enough to follow him?

Reflect and respond

1. How can you be prepared for the attacks of Satan against your faith?
2. What scares you the most about the idea of denying yourself, taking up your cross, and following Jesus?
3. What excites you the most about the idea of denying yourself, taking up your cross, and following Jesus?

God my Redeemer,
Thank you for Jesus.
Thank you that he humbled himself to death on a cross.
Thank you that he did it all out of love for me!
Lord, I want the true life and joy that you're offering.
I want to learn how to deny myself.
I want to trust your plan and follow wherever you lead me.
Please give me the courage to follow you even if it costs me everything.
Be my Lord and my God, my rock and my refuge.
Be my everything.

In Jesus' name,
Amen

Meditation verse for the day:

Whoever wants to be my disciple must
deny themselves and take up their cross
and follow me.
(Mark 8:34)

Day 25

The Transfiguration

(READ MARK 9:1-29)

TODAY WE GET TO read about a really incredible moment. Jesus and his three closest friends are up on a high mountain, when Jesus suddenly starts shining brightly with a blinding whiteness. In this miraculous moment, the disciples are getting a glimpse into who Jesus really is. They are being shown a tiny preview of what heaven will be like, where the glory of God the Father and God the Son will shine brighter than the sun. Hebrews 1:3 tells us, "The Son is the radiance of God's glory and the exact representation of his being." This means that Jesus is God. God's glory is Jesus' glory. Jesus is literally shining with the radiant glory of God himself.

The glory of God

So the next question we need to ask ourselves is, what exactly is God's glory? It's a word we hear a lot, but do we actually know what it is? How would you describe God's glory? The best answer is to look at how God defines it in Exodus 33 and 34. Moses asks God directly, "Please show me your glory," and God agrees and says, "I will cause all of my goodness to pass in front of you, and I will proclaim my name, the Lord, in your presence" (Exodus 33:19). It's so striking that Moses asks to see God's *glory*, and God responds by showing Moses his *goodness*. To God, they're the same thing! And as he shows Moses a little glimpse of his glory, God announces who he is:

> "The Lord, the Lord, the compassionate and gracious God, slow to anger, abounding in love and faithfulness, maintaining love to thousands, and forgiving wickedness, rebellion and sin. Yet he does not leave the guilty unpunished; he punishes the children and their children for the sin of the parents to the third and fourth generation" (Exodus 34:6–7).

Keep in mind that this is happening straight after God's chosen people have broken their covenant (promise) with him by worshipping a golden calf idol. God is saying to Moses that his glory is best seen in the goodness he shows to people who have rejected him. His glory is his compassion and his grace toward sinners. His glory is his patience and his abounding love and his faithfulness when his people aren't faithful to him. His glory is his willingness to forgive. His glory is also in his holy and righteous judgment of sin. In God's own words, the best way he shows his glory is this: that he lovingly showers mercy and grace on sinners. How encouraging is that?

Beholding the glory of God

The New Testament tells us that when we look at Jesus, we see God's glory. When we see how Jesus lives, we're seeing God's glory in action. Jesus is the glory of God in a living, breathing human body! When Jesus loves outcasts and sinners and Pharisees, that's God's glory. When Jesus is abounding in mercy to the very people who are killing him, that is God's glory. When Jesus forgives and is slow to anger even when people whip him and spit in his face, that's the glory of God shining through.

We don't spend enough time thinking about the glory of God. We read about Jesus but it doesn't always lead us to fall down on our faces before him in worship. We know lots about who God is, but we don't always leave his presence changed, shining with his radiance inside and out. I want to encourage you to commit the rest of your life to dwelling on God's glory in Jesus Christ, more and more each day. You won't be wasting a single moment. Practice delighting in the beauty of his compassion. Learn how to bask in the generosity of his patience. Marvel at his rock-solid faithfulness. Celebrate his forgiveness in awe and wonder. Tremble at his holy hatred of sin. Don't let him become so familiar that your thoughts about him become ordinary and small. Linger over the Bible, enjoying Jesus and asking the Holy Spirit to thrill your heart with his excellence and worthiness. Every time you open God's word, pray for him to show you his glory! Read

Bible-centered books about who God is, to help you see his majesty more clearly. One of my favourites is Adam Ramsey's *Truth on Fire*.

Sanctification

God promises that as we devote ourselves to gazing at his glory, he transforms us to be like Jesus (2 Corinthians 3:18). Lingering over God's glory is how we become glorious. Meditating on his compassion and grace and love and mercy is how we become radiant with his goodness. This process of being transformed to be like Jesus is called *sanctification* and it begins when we're first saved and continues on for the rest of our lives. Sanctification is actually how we become who we already are. Let me repeat that: Sanctification is *how you become who you already are.* That means you're *already* an adopted child of the King, and now he wants to help you start living like one. Jesus didn't die for you so that you could keep living like an orphan. He didn't die for you so that you could stay exactly the same person you were before you were saved. He wants you to experience the completeness of his freedom, and contentment, and rest. He wants you to grow radiant with God's glory; his loving, joyful, peaceful, patient and kind glory. He wants to fill you with all the fullness of himself! So fix your eyes on his glory and become who you already are: a joyful, love-radiating child of the King.

Reflect and respond

1. What do you find most beautiful and amazing about God's glory?
2. What's most precious to you about your adoption as God's child?
3. How are you still living and thinking like an orphan, instead of as a cherished child of God?

Turn in your Bible to Psalm 8. Pray this psalm to God today, savoring his majestic glory and the wonderful gift of his care for you.

Meditation verse for the day:

The Lord, the Lord, the compassionate and gracious God,
slow to anger, abounding in love and faithfulness,
maintaining love to thousands,
and forgiving wickedness, rebellion and sin.
Yet he does not leave the guilty unpunished.
(Exodus 34:6–7)

Day 26

Greatness in God's Kingdom

(Read Mark 9:30–50)

Servant of all

Jesus wants the disciples to see that God's vision for a good life is totally opposite to what they expect. He knows they're arguing amongst themselves about who deserves the most power and honor, so in verse 35 he gives them a hard truth: "Anyone who wants to be first must be the very last, and the servant of all." He's helping them understand what it really means to belong to God's family. He's reminding them that God's upside-down kingdom is actually all about putting aside our rights so that we can serve others. God's deepest desire for us isn't that we gain lots of power and privilege. God's desire for us is that we lay down our power and privilege to love God and our neighbors well.

This is so completely opposite to how the kingdom of this world works that it can be hard to wrap our minds around it! The world says to spend our lives striving for more money, more influence, more success, and more stuff. We're taught that the way to happiness is to put our own needs first. We're encouraged to fight for our rights, to be independent and free, and not to let anyone else hold us back from what we deserve. But look around: it doesn't really seem to be working. People are more depressed and lonely than ever. Jesus offers us a radically different path here. He invites us into a kingdom that's characterized by humility and servant-hearted love. God's heart is for his children to be selfless and generous, lovingly sacrificing ourselves for others. We serve a gentle King who gave up his life for the people who killed him. As his disciples, we're called to follow him. This is how we play our part in bearing witness to God's kingdom on earth as it is in heaven.

Cut off sin

Starting in verse 42, Jesus warns his disciples of the eternal dangers of sin. Some Christians today are uncomfortable talking about sin and hell because they don't want to seem judgmental. Jesus clearly didn't feel that way, because he talks about it in very strong language. There is absolutely no doubt how serious it is in his eyes. Jesus *hates* sin. He says here that hell is very real, and that it's a horrific place to end up. He also clearly explains that unless we all take radical and extreme action against the things that tempt us, we're in danger of spending eternity in hell. He believes this so passionately that he's using the dramatic examples of cutting off parts of our body to help us avoid sin. Jesus isn't actually encouraging us to hurt ourselves; he's using exaggeration to make a strong point. He obviously wants this warning to stick in our memories! Take a few moments now to re-read verses 43–48, to remind yourself just how deathly serious Jesus is here.

All of us are experts at pointing out sin in the lives of others, but in response to such a powerful warning, we'd be wise to urgently and honestly reflect on our own sin. Some Christians love talking about sin, as long as it's the sin of other people. It's really easy to look around at society and blame others for the mess we see. But remember, Jesus isn't warning us here about the sin in our neighborhoods or our schools or our cities. He's warning us about the sin in our own personal lives. He isn't asking us to judge or criticize others around us who are sinning. He's asking us to take a good, hard look at ourselves. Ask yourself right now: Is there sin in your life that you justify as just being part of your personality? Is there sin that you enjoy too much to resist it? Is there sin you've stopped fighting because it seems like you'll never beat it? Jesus is warning you about that sin today. Don't become comfortable or familiar with your sin. Don't let it settle down and grow roots in your life. Don't underestimate it. Don't let it creep up on you and gradually suffocate your faith. Arm yourself for battle, and be prepared to fight the darkness that's lurking inside you and around you.

Hell is a serious and challenging topic. If you want to know more about what the Bible says about hell, I strongly recommend reading *Erasing Hell* by Francis Chan and Preston Sprinkle.

Living out of God's power

Thankfully, God doesn't just leave us on our own to figure out how to do all these things. Following Jesus is never about trying harder. It's never about striving in our own strength, or fighting sin in our own power. That would just leave us constantly exhausted. Instead, Jesus generously gives us everything we need to be able to follow him. He calls us to be like him, and then he offers to make us like him. He tells us to obey, and then he helps us be able to obey. Peter explained it like this: "By his divine power, God has given us everything we need for living a godly life. We have received all of this by coming to know him," (2 Peter 1:3, NLT). God's divine Spirit is in you and he gives you *everything* you need to live a life that honors Jesus. How does this happen? Peter says it's through knowing God. Through our growing intimacy with him. He's talking about the process of sanctification that we read about yesterday. As we walk closely with Jesus and meditate on his glory daily, God's Spirit grows our character to be like his. When we depend on God, he equips us and strengthens us out of his unlimited power! So Jesus commands us to love our neighbor, and then the Holy Spirit transforms us to be more loving, more peaceful, more patient and kind, and more gentle. Jesus commands us to ruthlessly cut sin out of our lives, and then his Spirit helps us to hate our sin and to put to death our sinful desires. God is so passionate about making you holy. Depend on him to keep his word and make you like Jesus. Fix your heart on him and let him supernaturally change you from the inside out.

Reflect and respond

1. *What excites you most about belonging to God's kingdom instead of the kingdom of this world?*
2. *What challenges you most about the idea of becoming a servant of all?*
3. *What sin is the Holy Spirit leading you to repent for today?*

Turn in your Bible to the Lord's prayer in Matthew 6:9–13. Pray it out to God in your own words.

Meditation verse for the day:

Anyone who wants to be first
must be the very last,
and the servant of all.
(Mark 9:35)

Day 27

Divorce and Marriage

(Read Mark 10:1–16)

The divorce question

In verse 2 Jesus is asked a tricky question about divorce. These Pharisees are trying to test Jesus' interpretation of scripture and involve him in a local controversy about when divorce is allowed under Jewish law. But instead of getting involved in their debate, Jesus simply refocuses the conversation on what really matters. He goes right back to Creation and says, "Let me remind you what God's wonderful, perfect plan was for marriage before sinful people messed it all up."

Quoting Genesis, Jesus says that marriage is an incredibly unique and sacred relationship in God's eyes. God created marriage to be a commitment between one man and one woman, for the rest of their lives. He planned for marriage to be the start of a brand new family that takes first priority. He designed sex as a beautiful way of bringing two married people together so intimately that it's like they've become one person. When people get married, they've been joined together by God in an exclusive, permanent relationship. Marriage is a precious gift from God!

Marriage and sin

In just four simple verses, Jesus has spoken some truths that can sound pretty extreme in our modern ears. Maybe what Jesus says about marriage here feels hurtful or triggering to you. I know this is a topic that can involve a lot of heartache for many people. Jesus knows this too. In verse 5 he acknowledges that because of sin, God's best plan is not our current reality. Sin has brought pain into our relationships. Sin has corrupted our bodies and our minds and our desires. Sin has turned God's sacred gift of marriage into something that can bring lifelong hurt and intergenerational trauma. What we see in most of the romantic relationships around us right now isn't what God wants for us. This isn't his perfect design for human intimacy and joy. He never wanted love and sex and families to turn out like this, and it grieves him deeply.

It's also important to emphasize here that Jesus isn't telling anyone to stay in an abusive marriage. Even though divorce breaks his heart, verse 5 shows us that divorce is sometimes tragically necessary in this sinful world. Let's say it again to be clear: Jesus is not commanding you to stay in a relationship that's putting you at risk. He isn't honored by you losing your health or life by staying in a dangerous marriage. This can be a very complex, sensitive topic. If there's a lot of brokenness in your romantic relationship, or in your family history, or your experience of sex or sexuality, I encourage you to find someone spiritually mature and qualified to talk to, like a Christian therapist, godly mentor, or your pastor. And please know that God sees and cares about every single tear you've shed. He hates the sin that's led to your pain. This is not how it should be.

Maybe you feel like Jesus' words here are old-fashioned and irrelevant in our world where casual sex and divorce are so normal. Jesus' response in verse 6 is to point us back to Creation. He's reminding us that his vision of marriage doesn't come from tradition or culture or politics. Jesus says that this is the way God our Maker designed it to be from the very beginning of human existence, so it applies throughout history, to everyone, everywhere. God made men and women. God made marriage. God made love and romance. God made sex. God made families. All of these things are his ideas and his creations. That means that he alone has authority to define them and decide how they work best. They belong to him, and that's just as true today as it was way back in Genesis. For Christians, this means that our culture doesn't have the right to tell us what marriage means, only God does. Our feelings don't get to decide what sex is for, only God does.

The gift of marriage

It's very clear from this passage that marriage *really* matters to God. He created it to be something very special, set apart from all other human relationships. Marriage is part of what he looked at with joyful satisfaction on the sixth day of Creation and called "very good." This means that marriage should also really matter to us. We should take romantic love and sex very seriously. As a young person living in the modern world, this means that you need to find out what God says about marriage, instead of letting your perspective be shaped by the world around you. Even if marriage feels like it's a long way away for you, it's never too early to learn what God thinks. Don't idolize the relationships you see in movies and TV shows. Don't let your heart be tricked into believing that sex is meaningless. Don't trust your friends to tell you what true love looks like. Only God knows exactly what it takes for human relationships to flourish, because he's the one who made us and designed us. Let his word guide how you think about it, instead of just going along with whatever your culture happens to say is good and right in the moment. Find godly books to help you thoughtfully explore what the Bible teaches. I recommend John Mark Comer's *Loveology* to look at God's beautiful purpose for marriage, and Jackie Hill Perry's *Gay Girl, Good God* for an inspiring testimony of wrestling with sexuality from a biblical perspective. Let God's words on marriage saturate your thoughts and feelings, and ask his Spirit to help you trust that his plan for marriage really is very, very good.

Reflect and respond

1. *Who or what are the biggest influences on how you think about love, sex, and marriage?*
2. *Did any parts of what Jesus says here feel old-fashioned or offensive to you? Which parts, and why?*
3. *How will you make sure your understanding of marriage is shaped by God's eternal word, instead of the world's ever-changing values?*

God my Creator,
Thank you that you made men and women in your image, to love and be loved.
Thank you that you designed sex to bring a beautiful intimacy and oneness to marriage.
Thank you that you want families to be places of joy and safety.
Thank you that your plan for marriage is for our good.
Renew my thinking so that I can see the beauty of your original plan for marriage.
Help me to honor you in my romantic relationships.

In Jesus' name,
Amen

Meditation verse for the day:

But at the beginning of creation
God 'made them male and female.'
'For this reason a man will leave his father and mother
and be united to his wife,
and the two will become one flesh.'
So they are no longer two, but one flesh.
(Mark 10:6–8)

Day 28

The Rich and the Kingdom of God

(Read Mark 10:17-34)

This one of Jesus' most famous conversations. We might be familiar with what he says here about money and possessions, but if we're honest, how many of us have really wrestled with what it means for us personally? Have you actually let Jesus' words change the way you use your money? Take a moment now to pray for God's Spirit to teach, convict and help you through his word today. Pray for the courage and faith to act on what you learn.

Money as our god

The man who falls to the ground in front of Jesus in verse 17 seems to be on the right track spiritually. He's eager to be saved, and he lives a moral life. But Jesus sees his heart. He knows that what's standing between this man and God are his possessions. His earthly treasures are just too important to him, and they're holding him back from really putting his trust in God. So Jesus tells him to do something life-changing: sell everything and donate the money to the poor. The man is absolutely devastated, which is probably exactly how most of us would feel in this situation.

It's important to notice that Jesus is talking to one particular man here. He doesn't always ask every disciple to give away everything. But the point is, *he might*. The call to discipleship is always a call to give up whatever Jesus asks, as we follow him to wherever he leads. And often—for our own good—he'll ask us to give up the things that are standing in the way of our love for him. It might be our possessions, or a relationship, or a particular dream we have for the future. Jesus wants us to trust him to be enough for us, no matter what else we have to lose along the way.

Money in God's kingdom

Jesus' advice to this rich man is incredibly challenging. It goes against *everything* we think we know is true. Our entire modern world is set up to make money our god. We trust money for our safety and security. We hope in money for our future. We make our big life decisions around it. We depend on it to give us everything we think we need. We're willing to make huge sacrifices to get more of it. And this all seems completely normal to us. It's what's expected and celebrated and valued in our culture. But can you see how this encourages us to idolize money? This is exactly why Jesus says his famous line in verse 25 about how hard it is for rich people to enter the kingdom of God. He's warning us that money is seductive and dangerous, and we all need to wrestle thoughtfully with how we relate to it.

In a world that worships money, Jesus invites us to a way of life that's completely different on every possible level. Jesus is challenging us to hold earthly things lightly and to give them away happily, so that we can learn to trust him to provide for us. He wants us to experience how generous he is. In God's economy, the more we have, the more we can give. Our possessions are an opportunity to practice radical generosity. Money is simply a tool for loving and serving others.

Treasure that lasts

Some people teach that God wants us all to be wealthy and successful. They interpret the promise in verses 29 and 30 literally, but that makes no logical sense. Why would Jesus warn us about the dangers of earthly treasure and then straight away promise us more earthly treasure as a reward? He's actually saying that no matter what we give up for him, it won't end up feeling like a sacrifice. Even if we give up the things that are most precious to us, he'll give us spiritual treasure that will make it all worthwhile. He'll ultimately give us back far more than we ever let go of. Verse 21 is just so precious and encouraging: "Jesus looked at him and loved him." Jesus isn't trying to punish this man or make him miserable. He's saying all this in love. He's saying this to save him. He's warning that his trust in his earthly wealth is risking his eternal soul. This man's hands and heart are too full to hold onto spiritual treasure, and Jesus longs to free him up for something better. As pastor David Platt helpfully explains:

> "Jesus' words are not a call to sacrifice as much as they are a call to satisfaction. Sure, Jesus beckons the man to sell everything he has on earth, but in the next breath he promises the man everlasting treasure in eternity... In the end, Jesus is not calling this man *away from* treasure, he's calling him *to* treasure."[1]

Jesus doesn't ever promise to make us all rich in this life. But he does promise to give us more spiritual goodness than we could ever imagine. More of himself. More peace. More joy. More contentment. More life. More love. More fullness. More belonging. The question is, do you believe him? Will you put your money where your mouth is?

Please don't close this book without deciding how you're going to respond to Jesus' powerful words today. Don't just assume that Jesus is only talking to people with more money than you. Commit to living a simple, counter-cultural lifestyle that is radically dependent on God. Commit to using your money and possessions as a tool to generously bless others. If you'd like to think more deeply about what this means for your life, David Platt's wonderful book *Radical* is a helpful place to start.

Reflect and respond

1. *What do money and possessions mean to you? Are they central to your identity? Your security? Your self-worth? Your happiness? Your life goals?*
2. *If Jesus told you right now to give away everything you own, what would your response be?*
3. *How can you use your money to love your neighbors better?*

---

1. Platt, *Counter Culture*, 55.

Turn to Psalm 23 in your Bible, and pray it out to God.

Meditation verse for the day:
And my God will meet all your needs
according to the riches of his glory in Christ Jesus.
(Philippians 4:19)

Day 29

Bartimaeus

(READ MARK 10:35–52)

Honoring the least

JESUS IS TRAVELING THROUGH the town of Jericho, when a blind beggar called Bartimaeus tries to get his attention. Lots of the people in the crowd are yelling abuse at Bartimaeus. They obviously don't think he's worthy of Jesus' time, and are probably worried he'll annoy Jesus. They literally can't imagine that someone like Jesus would ever want to talk to someone like Bartimaeus. It's like a few verses ago in Mark 10:13, when people were bringing their little children to Jesus and the disciples tried to send them away. In both situations, Jesus welcomes in the exact people that everyone else is deliberately ignoring. Jesus gives his undivided attention to the people no one else thinks are worth the effort. He blesses the people everyone else sees as an inconvenience and an embarrassment. It's important that the story of Bartimaeus comes immediately after Jesus' teaching about serving others. Mark is deliberately reminding us that when Jesus says we have to be servants of all, he really does mean *all*. There are no exceptions.

Every culture throughout human history has judged and ranked people according to different values and priorities. A person's worth has been based on their wealth, or appearance, or education, or abilities, or age, or skin color, or immigration status, or the brand of clothing they wear. There are thousands of reasons why we look down on other people and tell ourselves we have more worth than them. Jesus smashes apart this way of thinking. By deliberately making time in his busy day to care for people like little children and blind beggars, he shows that there isn't a single person on earth who isn't equally valuable and precious in his eyes. Even the poorest, dirtiest beggar is made in God's image, and so they deserve to be treated in the same way as the King himself. The Bible repeatedly says we show our love for God by loving the people he made. If we're unloving towards *them*, we're actually rejecting *him*. This is what Jesus teaches us in Matthew 25:40, when he says, "Whatever you did for one of the least of these brothers and sisters of mine, you did for me." The way we welcome and serve poor, powerless, unlikeable people should be exactly the same way we would serve him personally. Jesus is challenging every single one of us to radically change how we see the people around us.

Think for a moment about the type of person you consider to be "the least" in your community. Be brutally honest with yourself. Who do you look down on? Who would you never want to be friends with? Who do you dismiss as being a lost cause? Who do you secretly feel like your community would be better off without? Jesus wants you to know that he adores those specific people. He looks at them and sees people created to reflect his majesty. People he deliberately knit together atom by atom. People he crowned with his glory. He believes they were worth dying for. And as his disciple, he wants you to treat those people with the exact same servant-hearted love that you would show to him personally. Pastor Jon Tyson says that in a world where it's so normal to express anger, contempt, disdain, and judgment toward anyone we don't like, God's people should stand out by showing honor to others instead. Tyson puts it simply and beautifully: "Honor is the culture of heaven."[1] We belong to a heavenly kingdom with a whole different way of valuing people. We don't only honor others if they meet certain standards. We don't only honor them once they've earned our respect. We don't only honor people who are nice to us, or who agree with us. We honor them because they bear the image of God himself. That alone gives them all the value they'll ever need. *Honor is the culture of heaven.* We have to let that truth deeply pierce our hearts and transform how we treat each other.

---

1. Tyson, *Beautiful Resistance*, 97.

You are loved

Young people around the world right now are struggling with sky-rocketing rates of depression and anxiety, and a deep sense of hopelessness and loneliness. Growing up is harder than it's ever been before in history. You are being attacked from every possible angle with accusations that you aren't good enough, aren't attractive enough, aren't popular enough, aren't successful enough. If that sounds like where you're at today, I'm so sorry.

Let Bartimaeus' story shine God's truth into your hurting heart. Let Jesus whisper his restoring love over your deepest pain. When others are rejecting you, he calls your name. When others are telling you that you don't belong, he pulls you close. He longs to gather you up in his arms and wipe all your tears away forever. He sees you and he delights in you. He rejoices over you with singing. He knows every single thing about you, and he genuinely enjoys you. Not because of how you look or what your grades are like or how many followers you have online. Not because of how hard you work or what other people think of you or how nice you are or how many goals you score. Not because of anything you've ever done or will ever do. You didn't earn his love by being good, and you can't lose his love by messing up. *He adores you simply because you're his.* You're infinitely precious to him because his fingerprints are on your soul. He made the greatest sacrifice for you, and he doesn't regret it for a moment. When you were lost, he searched high and low for you, so he could welcome you into his kingdom with songs of joy. You are a child of the Most High God, and you are so dearly loved.

Reflect and respond

1. *What excuses do you make to try and get out of generously serving others?*
2. *Think about a person you struggle to serve and honor in love. How might it help to remember they've been made in the image of God?*
3. *What truth about God has encouraged you today?*

Savior God,
There's no one like you!
I stand in awe of your kindness and love and compassion.
I want to serve and honor others, like Jesus.
Show me how I can draw nearer to the 'least of these' in my own community,
so that I can love them with your love.
Help me to see them through your eyes, as holy image-bearers of the Most High God.
Make me like you, so that I can care for them out of your abundant patience and kindness and gentleness.

In Jesus' name,
Amen

Meditation verse for the day:

Whoever wants to become great among you must be your servant,
and whoever wants to be first must be slave of all.
For even the Son of Man did not come to be served,
but to serve, and to give his life as a ransom for many.
(Mark 10:43–45)

Day 30

King Jesus

(Read Mark Chapter 11)

Entry into Jerusalem

It's nearly time for Passover, one of the biggest Jewish celebrations on the calendar. Just like every other year, Jesus heads into Jerusalem along with hundreds of thousands of other Jewish people who are traveling from all over the countryside. This year is different, though. This year, Jesus knows he's about to die. He's not heading to a celebration, he's heading to his death. The other difference this year is that Jesus rides into Jerusalem on a young donkey, with people lining up along the street to cheer for him. Laying cloaks and branches across the road was how the Israelites used to celebrate a new king in the Old Testament. We might think it's strange that Jesus suddenly has a huge crowd treating him like a king, but this didn't just happen out of nowhere. Jewish people had been desperately longing for their promised Savior for many generations. They knew that Zechariah had prophesied about the Christ five hundred years before:

> "See, your king comes to you,
> righteous and victorious,
> lowly and riding on a donkey,
> on a colt, the foal of a donkey" (Zechariah 9:9)

So when they see this miracle-working rabbi riding into the holy city, they must have felt overwhelmed with the exciting possibility that Jesus might finally be the Messiah they'd been waiting for all this time. They must have wondered if he was coming to take his place as king, and to fulfil all the wonderful Old Testament prophecies. In the parallel version of this account in Luke 19, when some Pharisees tell Jesus to shut the crowd up, he answers, "I tell you, if they keep quiet, the stones will cry out" (verse 40). This is such a significant moment in history that all of nature is bursting at the seams trying to contain its praise! No wonder indescribable hope is tingling through the hearts of everyone watching. The King is finally here!

In the temple courts

Starting in verse 15, we read about Jesus kicking people out of the temple courts and flipping over tables! It's the last thing we would expect from a man who's normally as gentle and humble as Jesus. So what's going on here? The key to understanding this scene is in verse 17, when Jesus accuses them of turning God's house into a "den of robbers." The temple is the place where God's people came to worship in his presence. It should be a place of reverence and honor, so Jesus is absolutely furious that people are using it as an opportunity to rip each other off. It's striking that both Mark and Matthew include the specific detail of Jesus forcing out the dove sellers. Poor people who came to the temple to offer a sacrifice couldn't afford a whole cow or a sheep, so they bought doves to sacrifice instead. Matthew and Mark are making it clear that Jesus is *particularly* angry about poor people being cheated and taken advantage of as they come to worship God.

Verse 17 also gives us another important clue about why Jesus is so angry. He says God's house is meant to be a "house of prayer for all nations." The part of the temple where all the trading and selling happened was the court of the Gentiles, which was the only part of the temple where non-Jewish people were allowed to go. There were literally tens of thousands of people in that courtyard, exchanging currencies to pay the temple taxes, and buying and selling and slaughtering hundreds of thousands of animals. Imagine the chaos! Pastor Tim Keller explains:

> "And this was the place where the Gentiles were supposed to find God through quiet reflection and prayer. Jesus' reaction to all this was to start throwing the furniture over. Imagine the leaders hurrying to him in panic: "What's going on? Why are you doing this?"

He quoted from the prophet Isaiah in reply: "My house will be called a house of prayer for all nations"—that is, for the Gentiles. We are told this amazed those who heard him. Why? For one thing, it was popularly believed that when the Messiah showed up he would purge the temple of foreigners. Instead, here is Jesus clearing the temple *for* the Gentiles—acting as their advocate. . . Jesus was challenging the sacrificial system altogether and saying that the Gentiles—the pagan, unwashed Gentiles—could now go directly to God in prayer."[1]

Back in the Old Testament, God originally created the temple and its sacrifices to make a way for unworthy people to come into his holy presence. The temple is meant to be the place where God and his people meet. Jesus is angry that the temple rules are now being used to take advantage of poor people and foreigners. They're being used to block people's access to God. This is the exact opposite of what God intended. So here we see Jesus doing what he loves to do best: making a way for all people to come to God.

Righteous anger

You might be uncomfortable with Jesus' anger here. You might wonder if he's sinning. But the Bible teaches us that God is *always* furious when it comes to confronting evil. Pastor Ray Ortlund helpfully describes God's anger at sin being like the "solemn determination of a doctor cutting away the cancer that's killing his patient."[2] God hates sin because it's killing his beloved creation from the inside out. He's angry at sin because it causes us to destroy ourselves and others. Jesus' anger here is holy and right, because it's anger at sin. It's appropriate to be angry when human traditions are keeping people away from God. It's appropriate to be angry at injustice towards vulnerable people, especially when it's done in the name of God. It's appropriate to be angry when the places that are meant to be welcoming people to God are actually blocking them from meeting with him. God's anger is always holy and right. We should be thankful he loves us so deeply that he refuses to just let sin destroy us.

Or maybe you find that this angry Jesus resonates deeply with you. Maybe you're a pretty angry person yourself, so you find it easier to connect with a table-flipping Jesus. Our society is incredibly divided right now.

---

1. Keller, *King's Cross*, 156–157
2. Ortlund, *Isaiah*, 102

There's a lot of anger and hatred, especially in the online world. And there is a lot of genuine evil to be angry about. But be very careful. Jesus' anger is righteous and holy, but ours is often not. Keep in mind that Jesus' expression of anger here is the exception to how he usually behaves. This is not how he relates to normal people out in the street every day. Jesus is not known for his tough love, he's known for being gentle and lowly. When we're angry, we need to ask the Holy Spirit to show us whether our anger is righteous. We need to check what we're really angry about deep down, and we need to be careful to express that anger without sinning. Remember, Jesus is angry at the powerful religious establishment for making it harder for people to come to God. He isn't angrily defending the Jewish nation or human traditions. He isn't angry at the immorality of Rome. He isn't angry at individual sinners making bad choices. He isn't angry about his own rights or preferences being taken away from him. He isn't belittling anyone or name-calling or typing violent messages at them online. Can you say the same about your anger?

Reflect and respond

1. What makes you angry?
2. What has this passage taught you about the kinds of things God gets angry about? Do you get angry at the same things as God does?
3. Why is God's anger at sin something to worship him for?

Turn in your Bible to Psalm 5, and make it your own prayer to God today.

Meditation verse for the day:

For you are not a God who is pleased with wickedness;
with you, evil people are not welcome...
But I, by your great love, can come into your house;
in reverence I bow down toward your holy temple.
(Psalm 5:4, 7)

Day 31

The Noble Vineyard Owner and His Son

(Read Mark 12:1–17)

Yesterday we read about Jesus burning with righteous anger. We read about him flipping over tables in the temple courts. We read about his fury at the injustice he sees there. Mark 11 ends with the religious leaders confronting Jesus and asking what authority he has to kick people out of the temple like that, and he refuses to respond to them directly. But then he tells a parable, which turns out to be an answer after all.

The parable of the tenants

The parable of the tenants actually tells the same story as the entire Bible. In verse 1, a man plants a vineyard, building it up from scratch. This represents God creating everything. He spoke the universe into being, weaving his creativity into every glorious detail, lovingly crafting it piece by piece. He made it all. He made us. Everything belongs to him. We are his.

In verse 2, the owner of the vineyard sends his servant to collect some of the fruit. This fruit is rightfully his, but the renters want to keep it all for themselves. This represents our rebellion against God. We take what's rightfully his, and pretend it's ours. We treat our lives as if they belong to us. We damage this planet as if it's our property. We make ourselves god. We absurdly think that if we just ignore him for long enough, we'll eventually rule our own lives. This is what sin is.

In verses 4 and 5, the vineyard owner sends more and more servants, but they keep getting beaten up or killed by the renters. This represents what we see happening all the way through the Old Testament up until John the Baptist, as prophet after prophet comes to warn people that their rebellion against God is going to end very badly. And time after time, the prophets get abused and chased out of town, or arrested and tortured, or even killed.

In verse 6, the vineyard owner decides to send his own son to the renters as a last resort, hoping they will respect him. Instead, in verses 7 and 8, they kill him. This represents the life of Jesus, whose death on a cross is now only a few days away. This is also Jesus' indirect answer to the religious leaders who were asking him what authority he has to force people out of the temple. He's saying to them, "I've been sent here by my Father. This temple belongs to him. I've come with his authority, so I have every right to do whatever I want here."

Verse 9 tells us that the vineyard owner has finally had enough. He kills the arrogant and evil farmers renting his vineyard, and gives it to new renters instead. This part of the parable represents the judgment that is coming. Jesus is warning us that how we respond to God *really* matters. How we respond to God's Son *really* matters. God's judgment is very real, and very serious. Will we keep rebelling against God and end up having everything taken away from us for all eternity? Or will we surrender ourselves to God, recognizing that we rightfully belong to him, and be saved? God doesn't want anyone to end up separated from him for eternity, but he will never force anyone to love him. So he invites us to choose for ourselves how we're going to respond to him. He patiently gives each of us lots of chances to decide, but these opportunities won't last forever. Eventually we'll run out of time. There will be judgment one day for every single one of us.

The parable of the noble vineyard owner

Kenneth Bailey, an expert in understanding the New Testament from an ancient Middle Eastern perspective, explains that this parable is carefully designed using a traditional Jewish literary structure. The original audience would have known this tradition and understood that the main point of the story is in the very middle, which is verse 6. Verse 6 tells us this: "He had

The Noble Vineyard Owner and His Son

one left to send, a son, whom he loved. He sent him last of all, saying, 'They will respect my son.'" *This* is the heart of Jesus' parable. This is the climax of his teaching. The core of the whole Bible story is that God sent us his beloved Son! This is what it's all about.

When we see that the focus of the parable isn't on the evil renters but on the vineyard owner and his beloved son, we read the whole parable through a different lens. We start to realize that God is the main character, and his actions in the story are the most important ones. And over and over again in this parable, what jumps out at us most about God is his extreme patience. He doesn't punish the renters immediately, even though he has every right to. Instead, he sends warning after warning, giving the people chance after chance to turn from their wickedness. Jesus is emphasizing how slow to anger God really is, even though people keep rejecting and dishonouring him. He graciously restrains his anger. He patiently waits to bring his righteous judgment on sin. He mercifully keeps trying to turn the evil people around, even though they don't deserve any more chances. And in the final shocking twist, he even puts everything he has on the line by sending his own beloved Son into danger, hoping to finally win them over. He becomes vulnerable for us. He chooses to lose everything for our sake. I can't even wrap my mind around such a level of undeserved grace! This parable is drenched in mercy. What a kind, patient God we have.

Reflect and respond

1. *What stands out to you most about God's character in this parable, and why?*
2. *How does this parable encourage you to worship God today?*

Most High God,
The earth is yours, and everything in it.
The world, and all who live in it belong to you.
You made everything. You made me. I'm yours.
You are my rightful Lord and King.
Thank you for your abundant patience with me.
Thank you for your overflowing grace.
Thank you for your kind mercy.
Thank you for sacrificing your beloved Son for me, even though I was your enemy.
I don't deserve any of it, but you delight in lavishing your grace on me because it's just who you are.
You are Love.
No one is like you Lord God.
My life is yours. I love you.

In Jesus' name,
Amen.

Meditation verse for the day:

The Lord isn't really being slow about his promise,
as some people think.
No, he is being patient for your sake.
He does not want anyone to be destroyed,
but wants everyone to repent.
(2 Peter 3:9, NLT)

Day 32

Love the Lord your God

(Read Mark 12:18–34)

The greatest commandment

In verses 29–30 Jesus says that the most important commandment in the whole Bible is, "The Lord our God, the Lord is one. Love the Lord your God with all your heart and with all your soul and with all your mind and with all your strength." This commandment was originally given to the Israelites while they were wandering around in the desert for forty years. These verses from Deuteronomy are called the *Shema*, and devout Jewish people have recited them every single morning and evening since the times of ancient Israel. It's one of the central prayers of their faith. As a Jewish man, Jesus himself would have prayed it every day of his life, and many modern Jewish people still do it to this day. Isn't that a beautiful tradition?

Jesus says that loving God is literally the best and most worthwhile thing we could ever spend our lives on. It should be the center of our existence. It should be our main priority, the thing that we pour all the best of our time and attention and effort into. Notice that the word "all" is repeated four times in just one sentence, which tells us it's really important! And the list of all the parts of ourselves we should love God with—our heart and soul and mind and strength—is pretty much just another way of saying *with every single part of us!* We should love God with our whole mind and spirit and body. With all our creativity and our passions and our sexuality and our skills. We should love God wholeheartedly, completely and utterly and supremely, with everything we have and everything we are.

A non-Christian friend of mine once joked that Christian worship music just sounds like love songs to Jesus. She's right! But that's nothing new. The psalms have been the main Jewish and Christian songs and prayers for thousands of years, and they're filled with passionate expressions of love. They teach us what it looks like to be deeply in love with God. Look at David's adoring language in Psalm 63:1–8:

> "God—you're my God! I can't get enough of you!
> I've worked up such a hunger and thirst for God,
> traveling across dry and weary deserts.
> So here I am in the place of worship, eyes open,
> drinking in your strength and glory.
> In your generous love I am really living at last!
> My lips brim praises like fountains.
> I bless you every time I take a breath;
> My arms wave like banners of praise to you.
> I eat my fill of prime rib and gravy;
> I smack my lips. It's time to shout praises!
> If I'm sleepless at midnight,
> I spend the hours in grateful reflection.
> Because you've always stood up for me,
> I'm free to run and play.
> I hold onto you for dear life,
> and you hold me steady as a post." (MSG)

David genuinely finds God breathtakingly captivating. He deeply enjoys God, and he knows that adoring God is the greatest thing he can do with every thought and breath. We should pray every day for David's words to become the song of our hearts too.

But how?

It can sound really weird to be commanded to love. Most modern cultures teach us that love is just something that happens to us: We fall in and out of love and just can't help ourselves. But the Bible commands us to love, so how do we do it? Can we really choose to love?

I find it helpful to think of how I fell in love with my husband. We got to know each other as friends in college. There was no particular romantic spark at the beginning, but the more time I spent with him and the more

I got to know him, the more the attraction grew. I watched how he treated other people, and learned about his character and his personality and his values and his choices, and I really liked what I saw. As we spent more time together, love started to blossom. We chose to keep spending time together, and we both committed to growing and protecting our relationship. We stopped looking at other crushes and gave all our attention to each other. We deliberately nurtured our love. And decades later, we still keep choosing to prioritize each other every day. And even now I just keep getting to know him better and better, and falling in love with him more and more!

My love for God is like my love for my husband. I can't force it, but I can live in a way that encourages it to grow and flourish. I can choose to spend quality time with God day after day, month after month, year after year. I can't really love God if I don't actually know who he is. And I don't have any right to make up who I want him to be. I need to invite him to tell me who he is, and listen carefully to what he says. God is God, and he tells us who he is in the Bible. So we should pour over his word, savoring every detail, treasuring it because his thoughts and ways are important to us. As we learn about his character, a little fire of love will be lit in our hearts. The more we prioritize him, the more opportunities there are for real love to grow. The more deeply we know him, the more deeply we'll love him.

God doesn't command us to love him because he likes giving us rules. He isn't trying to burden us. He knows that enjoying him is actually the key to finding deep and lasting joy. Loving God with all our heart and soul and mind and strength is literally what we were created for. It's the best, most satisfying thing we'll ever do. It's where fullness of joy is found. It's the deepest meaning of life.

Reflect and respond

1. *What emotions do you feel towards God? Do you love him?*
2. *How does today's passage challenge you to read the Bible differently?*
3. *What are three ways you can practice enjoying God more this week?*

Loving God,
Thank you for loving me so deeply.
I pray that the words David wrote 3000 years ago in Psalm 63 would become my words too.
I long to never be able to get enough of you.
I long to hunger and thirst for you.
I long to enjoy gazing at you, drinking in your strength and glory.
I long to feel truly alive in your love.
I want lips that can't stop gushing your praises.
I want to bless you with every breath I take.
When I'm lying sleepless in my bed, remind me to fix my mind on you.
Help me hold onto you as if my life depends on it.
Teach me how to really love you, with all my heart and soul and mind and strength.

In Jesus' name,
Amen

Meditation verse for the day:

Love the Lord your God
with all your heart
and with all your soul
and with all your mind
and with all your strength.
(Mark 12:30)

Day 33

Love Your Neighbor

(Read Mark 12:28–34)

What is love?

To understand what Jesus means when he tells us to love our neighbors as ourselves, we need to figure out what he means by the word 'love'. In the Bible's most famous passage about love, Paul explains:

> "Love is patient, love is kind. It does not envy, it does not boast, is it not proud. It does not dishonor others, it is not self-seeking, it is not easily angered, it keeps no record of wrongs. Love does not delight in evil but rejoices with the truth. It always protects, always trusts, always hopes, always perseveres" (1 Corinthians 13:4–7).

These verses show us that biblical love isn't only about feelings, it's actually mainly about *actions*. But it's not grand gestures like special gifts or expensive surprises; it's little selfless actions day in and day out like patience and gentleness and forgiveness. This kind of love lays down our own rights and desires, and puts other people first. This kind of love treats other people better than they deserve. It works tirelessly for their good, no matter what it costs. It protects and stands up for them. It doesn't hold grudges when they've hurt us. It sticks around when everyone else has given up hope. It speaks the truth in a way that is kind and honoring and humble. Pastor Eugene Peterson gives this wise insight:

"A dictionary is worthless in understanding and practicing love. Acts of love cannot be canned and then used off the shelf. Every act of love requires creative and personal giving, responding and serving appropriate to... both the person doing the loving and the person being loved."[1]

Peterson is saying here that loving someone is always personal, always unique, always tailored to a specific person in a particular situation. This means I don't show my grandma love in the exact same way as I do to my six-year old son. And how I show love to my sister when she's just had a baby might be different to how I showed her love when she was back in high school. To love my neighbor well, I need to really know them so that I can love them in a way that's meaningful to them in that moment.

Who is my neighbor?

The second thing we need to figure out here is who exactly Jesus means by "neighbor." When he's asked that exact question in Luke 10:29, Jesus replies with the parable of the Good Samaritan. This story teaches us that our neighbors are the people God puts around us; the people in our homes and on our street and in our classes and at our jobs. Even if they're people we have nothing in common with. Even if loving them is really inconvenient. Even if they're just not very nice people. Even if the world tells us we should be enemies with them. Notice that this command doesn't come with any conditions that we might use to try and wriggle out of it. Jesus doesn't say to only love people who deserve it. He doesn't limit it to just the people who we like, or who treat us with respect. "Just 'love your neighbour as yourself.' Period. Just do it whether you feel like it or not, whether you get anything out of it or not... God loves you. Christ shows you how love works. Now you love. Love, love, love, love. Just do it."[2] Take a moment to think about what that means in your own life. Who are the people God has put around you? Who are your neighbors?

This kind of self-sacrificing love doesn't seem logical or feel comfortable. Like we've seen before with the way of Jesus, it goes against everything the world tells us is best for us. Modern culture teaches us to prioritize ourselves and put our own needs and desires above anything else in life. Jesus says to put others first. Hollywood teaches us to only love other people if it makes us feel happy. Jesus says to love others even if they hurt us. Politicians

---

1. Peterson, *Kingfishers*, 40
2. Peterson, *Kingfishers*, 39, 41

tell us we need to fight against our enemies for the survival of our way of life. Jesus tells us to cross the battle lines and voluntarily lay down our way of life for them. We belong to the kingdom of God, not the kingdom of this world. Costly, selfless love is at the heart of our King and the culture of our kingdom. Our Savior Jesus died for us while we were his enemies. Our loving Father sacrificed his beloved Son for us while we were rebelling against him. Our God loves us when we're at our worst, when there's nothing we can bring to the relationship ourselves, and when there's no chance we'll ever be able to repay him. As his children, we have the responsibility and the privilege to do the same thing.

A big trap we can fall into when we try to obey this command, is to think that Jesus is calling us to be best friends with everyone, everywhere, all the time. But Jesus doesn't say, "Love your entire neighborhood," he simply says, "Love your neighbor." It's not humanly possible to love a huge number of people at the same time. You'll burn out. Jesus was filled to the brim with the power of the Holy Spirit, but even he didn't try to be everything for everyone. He chose just twelve people to build deep relationships with, and had an inner circle of three disciples he was closest to. God made us human, with human limitations. We can't save the whole world, but that's ok because saving the world is not our responsibility. Our responsibility is to faithfully love the handful of people God brings across our daily path.

Remember, *real love happens inside real relationships*. To love someone, you need to know them, and that always takes time and effort. So put your phone down and practice being radically present to the people God has put around you. Pay attention. Listen to their heart, and pray that God would teach you how to love them well. And don't worry if you feel like you aren't changing the world. In a world where everyone wants to be famous or powerful, author Andy Crouch encourages us to be content with keeping our influence small and local. He writes, "Love is a fragile thing that does not scale well. It seems small beside the towers of Babel and Babylon. It is like a mustard seed, tiny and seemingly vulnerable. But it is the unseen truth of the universe, the key to the whole story."[3]

How do we love like this?

What Jesus is saying here can feel a bit overwhelming. Because let's be honest: It's literally impossible for any of us to obey this command on our own.

---

3. Crouch, *Culture Making*, 248

Loving people well is *hard*. Thankfully, being a disciple of Jesus is never about trying more or working harder. We need some serious supernatural help, which is exactly what God promises to give us. Remember sanctification? Sanctification is the way that the Holy Spirit slowly transforms us to be more like Jesus as we get to know God better. It's a life-long process, so it doesn't mean we'll be perfect. It doesn't mean obeying God's commands will suddenly be easy. But it does mean that as our faith matures, loving others well becomes more and more natural to us. It means that as the Spirit bears his fruit in our hearts, we'll gradually become more loving, joyful, peaceful, patient, kind, good, faithful, gentle, and self-controlled toward the people around us.

Pastor Dane Ortlund has a great book called *How Does God Change Us?* which includes an important chapter about this transforming work that the Spirit does in our hearts. He says,

> "Keep in step with the person of the Holy Spirit. Ask the Father to fill you with the Spirit. Look to Christ, in the power of the Spirit. Open yourself up to the Spirit. Consecrate yourself to the beautiful Spirit's ways in your life. . . As you do so, you will be a little walking portrait of heaven itself to everyone around you. With lots of foibles and mistakes, for sure. . . But here and there, at first for short bursts but gradually for longer stretches of your day, you will be learning to operate out of God's own divine resources. You will be giving people a taste of Jesus himself, the Lord whose Spirit has taken up residence within you."[4]

Oh, I want so deeply to be a little picture of heaven walking around my community, don't you? What a gift it would be for our families and friends and neighbors to taste and see Jesus' love through us!

Reflect and respond

1. *How can you practice opening yourself up to God's Spirit, so that you love your neighbors in his strength instead of your own?*
2. *Who are the neighbors God has given you to love?*
3. *How can you practice being more fully present to one of those neighbors this week?*

---

4. Ortlund, *God Change Us*, 83–84

Love Your Neighbor

Merciful Father,
You sacrificed your beloved Son for me when I was still your enemy.
You poured out your incredible love on me, when I was doing my best to run away from you.
You invited me to become your child, when there was nothing I could give you in return.
You are love.
Your kingdom overflows with kindness and mercy and forgiveness and grace.
Help me see the needs of the people around me so that I can respond in love.
Give me eyes to see my neighbors the way you see them.
Teach me how to love them the way that you've loved me.
Make me more like you.

In Jesus' name,
Amen

Meditation verse for the day:

Love your neighbor as yourself.
(Mark 12:31)

Day 34

The Widow's Offering

(READ MARK 12:35-44)

Two small coins

THE STORY IN VERSES 41–44 about the poor widow is short, but it's so beautiful. This woman is a nobody in her community. She's a poor woman without a husband, in a society that values men, money, and marriage. She has no power or status. She has nothing to give. She's the exact opposite to the teachers of the law Jesus warns about in verses 38–40, who are respected everywhere they go. Yet Jesus looks at this woman and is deeply honored by the fact that she "put in everything—all she had to live on" (verse 44). Her sacrificial giving is a love offering, an act of worship. She's putting her money where her heart is, giving generously to the God she adores. She loves him so much that she wants to give him everything she has. She trusts him to provide for her needs, so she doesn't hold anything back.

This wonderful story teaches us so much about what matters most to God. He doesn't care about what the world thinks of us. He doesn't care about the exact dollar amount we give. What he cares about is our heart. What he cares about is *why* we give, and whether everything we do is motivated by love for him and for others. Like this poor widow, we honor God when we value him more than the things we own. We honor him when we recognize that everything we have is a gift from him in the first place. We honor him when our hearts are so filled with gratitude that we can joyfully give away our stuff. We honor him when we love our neighbors with the things he's given us, instead of hoarding it all greedily for ourselves. You might think you have barely anything to offer to God, whether it's money or time or skills. But Jesus tells us here that he wants everything we have, whether it's a lot or a little. You can trust him with all you are and all you have. He's worthy of it all. Are you holding anything back from him?

Stewardship

This story reminds us that everything we do matters to God. Even how we use money is actually a spiritual issue. The Bible teaches us that everything we have is a gift from God, and we're just stewards of it. A steward is someone who is temporarily responsible for looking after something that belongs to someone else. They know it isn't theirs. They know they don't have a right to do anything they like with it. Stewards invest and protect money in a way they know would please the owner, because one day they'll be held accountable for every cent that was in their care. That's a pretty different way of thinking about the stuff we own! When you plan out your future, do you think of your money as something that will belong to you, or that belongs to God? Do you feel like it's your right to spend your money however you want, or do you enjoy generously sacrificing it out of love for God and others? Does it scare you to think that one day God will hold you accountable for how you spent the money he generously blessed you with?

So what does God want us to spend our money on? How can we be good stewards of everything we own? The book of Acts tells the story of the first Christian churches after Jesus' death and resurrection, and it gives us a beautiful answer to that question. Acts 4:32–35 says,

> "No one claimed that any of their possessions was their own, but they shared everything they had... And God's grace was so powerfully at work in them all that there were no needy persons among them. For from time to time those who owned land or houses sold them, brought the money from the sales and put it at the apostles' feet, and it was distributed to anyone who had need."

This is what it can look like when we commit to living out the two great commandments of Jesus above all else. Here are people who love God so deeply that they've been freed from their love of money and freed from the fear of not having enough. They're people who love their neighbors so much that they're willing to sell their land and houses to support each other. This is costly, sacrificial love. This is good stewardship. And if it sounds too extreme to even be possible, there actually are communities of Christians around the world today who are committed to living together with this kind of radical generosity. I highly recommend reading Shane Claiborne's wonderful book *The Irresistible Revolution* if you're interested in finding out more.

Pastor David Platt has written a lot of practical advice on how we can steward our money in ways that honor God. In his challenging book *Counter Culture*, he says:

> "The Bible teaches that God gives us more not so that we can *have* more but so that we can *give* more... When we really grasp this, it will change the way we live. Practically, we set a cap on our lifestyle, determining a level of "enough" beyond which we are free to use the excess for the sake of others. Much like Paul, we prayerfully look at our possessions and say, "With this we will be content." Then, if or when we receive additional money, instead of that money increasing our standard of living, it only increases our standard of giving."[1]

Platt encourages us to live simply and to practice being content with less, to budget for generosity, and to pay attention to the needs that exists all around us. This is something every single one of us can start today, no matter how little we have in our bank account. Whatever you do, don't think this doesn't apply to you. Remember, the poor widow in today's passage gave just two small coins. Begin with what you have, as a love offering to your extravagantly generous Father. Give in humble worship of the One who gave everything for you.

Reflect and respond

1. *What do you spend your money on? What do you dream of spending money on in the future?*
2. *What does your spending show about what your heart treasures most?*
3. *What needs to change about your attitude towards money? How can you honor God with the money he's given you?*

---

1. Platt, *Counter Culture*, 43

The Widow's Offering

Generous Father,
You are my Maker, and the Lord of creation.
Everything I have is a gift from you. Thank you!
Please set me free me from loving money, so that I can be joyfully generous.
Thank you that you've promised to provide everything I need.
Teach me to trust you.
Open up my eyes to see the needs around me.
Help me to generously love my neighbors with what you've given me.
I want to honor you with how I think about my possessions.

In Jesus' name,
Amen

Meditation verse for the day:

"They all gave out of their wealth;
but she, out of her poverty,
put in everything—all she had to live on."
(Mark 12:44)

Day 35

Be Ready!

(READ MARK CHAPTER 13)

Be on your guard

THIS IS A HARD and confusing chapter to read. Jesus is actually talking on a few different levels at once. He's prophesying about the destruction of Jerusalem and the temple (which ended up happening in 70 AD), as well as prophesying about the end of the world. But at the heart of Jesus' message in this chapter is the warning he repeats over and over: *Be on your guard! Be alert! Keep watch! Stay awake!* So what exactly does this mean for us?

There are Christians who are obsessed with thinking about the end of the world. They try to analyze the prophecies in the Bible to predict exactly when Judgment Day will come. But this is definitely not what Jesus is telling us to do in this passage. In fact, in verse 32 he warns us that it would be a complete waste of our time, because "about that day or hour no one knows, not even the angels in heaven, nor the Son, but only the Father." No matter how hard we try, we'll never be able to predict when the end of the world will happen. When it comes, it will surprise everyone.

Jesus *is* talking about the end times here, but he's *not* encouraging us to obsess over the specific details of when or how. He says it's definitely going to happen, and it's coming closer. One day, life as we know it will end. One day Jesus the Judge will come back, radiant with power and glory, and everyone on earth will bow before him. But maybe that's as much as we really need to know about it. It doesn't need to scare us. But it also isn't something we should ignore, because it's actually really important! Our responsibility is to stay ready for it to happen at any time.

Jesus explains how we stay ready in verse 34. "It's like a man going away: He leaves his house and puts his servants in charge, each with their own assigned task, and tells the one at the door to keep watch." We're Jesus' servants in this scenario, and he gives every single one of us an assigned task to do before he comes back. We've each been created for a reason. Your life has a sacred purpose. You're literally still alive right now because you haven't finished whatever God put you on this earth for.

I can't tell you exactly what your assigned task is, because it's unique to you. Your specific role is different from every single other person who's ever lived in the history of the world! You're going to have to prayerfully listen to the Holy Spirit to find out where he's leading you and what he's calling you to do. But the Bible does tell us very clearly what the general purpose is for every single Christian, which is to glorify God and enjoy him forever. The whole point of our lives is that Jesus Christ is exalted and delighted in. That he gets the honor and glory he deserves. That we find our fullness of joy in him. Our short lives have huge eternal significance when they show the world how awesome God is. And we have the most joy when we focus our lives on adoring him! That's what it's all about.

Living in the kingdom of God

As a mother, I love that in verse 8 Jesus calls all of the terrible wars and famines "the beginning of birth pains." Giving birth is really hard. But when a woman is in labor, each painful contraction is actually an encouraging sign that a baby is a tiny bit closer to being born. Labor pains mean a new life is almost here. Can you feel the anticipation fizzing through this metaphor? It whispers, *Something new and wonderful is coming!* When Jesus came to earth, he brought the kingdom of God to us. But this kingdom won't be fully here until he comes back a second time, at the end of the world. Like a woman in labor, all of creation is groaning in pain, waiting eagerly for the new life that's on its way. We all long for God's kingdom to come in full and bring an end to all of the suffering and sin on this earth. But we live in the time in between. We're living in the labor pains that are bringing in the reign of our glorious King. One day God's kingdom will be announced with trumpets and angels and radiant heavenly glory, but right now we live in the tiny mustard seed kingdom; slowly sprouting roots and leaves, quietly becoming a home to anyone who comes to find shelter and safety and peace in its humble branches.

But we don't have to wait for heaven to live in God's kingdom. As Christians, we actually already live there! Our souls are already safe with Jesus in heaven (Ephesians 2:6). Jesus taught us to pray that God's kingdom would come on earth, just like in heaven. Our lives are part of the answer to that prayer. When we love God and our neighbors, we show that another way of life is possible. We're witnesses to what it means to live in a new kingdom that has a culture of love and honor and gentleness and goodness and hope. When our lives are a love song to Jesus, we bring a taste of heaven to the hurting world around us. *This* is how we exalt Jesus through our lives, showing that he is who he says he is. The world is watching us as we represent our King. What will they see? Do our lives show that God's kingdom is wonderfully real? Are we living proof that heaven is breaking into earth? Do we look more and more like Jesus with every month and year that passes? If you aren't sure where to start, look for all the places in the Gospels where Jesus talks about the kingdom of God or the kingdom of heaven. He has a *lot* to say about it. Ask the Holy Spirit to shape you inside and out with Jesus' words, and to grow the fruit of his kingdom in your own life. I also encourage you to read Jen Wilkin's wonderful book *Ten Words to Live By*, which teaches us what it looks like to live holy lives as citizens of God's kingdom, playing our part in inviting heaven to come on earth.

Jesus warns us in Mark 13 to be alert and to stay awake. When he comes back, the kingdom of this earth will be over forever, and the kingdom of God will have arrived in fullness. Before that day, our job is to be like a beautiful fragrance, sweetly filling the world around us with the goodness and majesty of Jesus Christ. Our job is to enjoy God deeply and richly, and to let our joy leak out into the lives of the people around us! Don't miss out on the privilege of loving others into the kingdom of God. Don't let Jesus come back and find you living like the kingdom of earth is all there is.

Reflect and respond

1. How do the truths of this chapter change how you think about the purpose of your life?
2. Do you live like you're a citizen of the kingdom of heaven, or like the kingdom of this world is all there is?
3. How is God calling you to live like a citizen of heaven today?

Turn in your Bible to Psalm 145. Prayerfully read it out as your song of praise to God your King.

Meditation verse for the day:

"I raised you up for this very purpose,
that I might display my power in you
and that my name might be proclaimed in all the earth."
(Romans 9:17)

Day 36

Jesus Anointed at Bethany

(Read Mark 14:1–11)

Extravagant love

This is an absolutely stunning story. A woman takes some very expensive perfume and pours it over Jesus while he's at a dinner party. The parallel version of the event in John 12 tells us that the woman is Mary, the sister of Martha and Lazarus, and that her perfume is worth a year's salary. Some of the people watching criticize her in very strong language. They argue that Mary's act of worship is excessive. They try to shame her for wasting something so valuable. But in verse 6 Jesus defends her, saying, "She has done a beautiful thing to me." He says it's totally appropriate. He dignifies her by gladly accepting her sacrifice and publicly honoring her.

This is a story of extravagant love. Mary *loves* Jesus. She's pledging her full allegiance to Jesus, in front of everyone, without caring what they think of her. She's willing to put her money where her mouth is, joyfully sacrificing something very precious to show her adoration. Her only priority is to honor Jesus and express her love for him. Her heart longs for him. She won't settle for anything less that being in his presence. And when she's with him, she can't help but worship him with the very best she has to give. She knows that the best thing in all of life is to be with her beloved and to love him the way he deserves. She wisely knows that this is exactly what she was created for. It's the kind of extravagant love *you* were created for too.

Don't you want to experience that kind of heart-bursting passion? You long for a powerful, deep love because it's how God made you. He put that desire inside you because it's the kind of love he wants to give you. You weren't made for anything less than extravagant love for the one who loves you best. This is a relationship that should be on fire, bursting at the seams with rejoicing and wonder and delight! Loving and being loved by our beloved is what every single person on the planet is searching so hard for. But often we settle for so much less. We coast through our days, scrolling on our phones and being distracted and entertained by meaningless things. Or we pour our deepest love into things that will never fully satisfy us: sport teams, or romantic relationships, or careers. That's how you waste your life. That's how you waste your passion. The philosopher C.S. Lewis famously wrote: "Our desires [are] not too strong, but too weak. We are half-hearted creatures, fooling around with drink and sex and ambition when infinite joy is offered us, like an ignorant child who wants to go on making mud pies in a slum because he cannot imagine what is meant by the offer of a holiday at the sea. We are far too easily pleased."[1] Don't settle. Don't let yourself be too easily pleased. God has made you for "an inexpressible and glorious joy" (1 Peter 1:8). He's made you for a relationship of abundant, extravagant passion with the God who is Love. Are you in?

Cultivating extravagant love

But how do we love Jesus the way Mary does? We find our answer in Luke 10, which tells the story of Jesus visiting Mary's sister's home. Mary's sister Martha is running around busily getting everything ready for Jesus, and is frustrated with her sister for not helping her around the house. Instead, Mary is simply sitting at Jesus' feet, listening. When Martha asks Jesus to tell Mary off, Jesus replies, "Martha, Martha. . . You are worried and upset about many things, but few things are needed—or indeed only one. Mary has chosen what is better, and it will not be taken away from her" (Luke 10:41-42). Martha isn't doing a bad thing; she's trying to honor Jesus by serving him. But Mary is just enjoying Jesus. She's basking in his presence, savoring his words. She's at his feet, where his disciples sit, even though that wasn't culturally appropriate for a woman. She doesn't want to miss anything he says, so she prioritizes being with him over anything else. She gives him her time and her full attention. And Jesus honors her by saying

---

1. Lewis, *The Weight of Glory*, 2.

that she's doing the best thing she could possibly do. And it's the same for us. The best thing we could ever do with our time each day is to make space to just be with him. To drink in what he says. To feel his presence. To tune out everything else around us and simply gaze on him. *This* is how we grow to love him like Mary.

I really appreciate pastor Tim Chester's book *Enjoying God*, because he encourages us to see that loving God is a spiritual muscle. We need to keep training that muscle, practicing enjoying God regularly so that it grows strong and stays strong. He helpfully explains that loving God isn't what saves us, because our salvation is a free gift from God that isn't based on anything we do. But enjoying and loving God does hugely affect *how we experience God*. Chester gives the example of a father with two sons, Phil and Jack. Phil avoids their father and barely interacts with him, but Jack talks to their dad lots and they regularly hang out together. He writes,

> "How many sons does the father have? The answer, of course, is two. And what did they do to become sons? Nothing. They were simply born as sons. But only Jack enjoys being a son. Only Jack experiences a good relationship with his father. Praying and reading your Bible won't make you more Christian. And not doing these things won't make you less of a Christian. . . Our status as God's children is a gift. But how much we enjoy that communion depends on what we do."[2]

Loving someone who loves us back is the most glorious experience of being human. The great tragedy is that some Christians miss out on the wonder of bursting with love for the God who feels the same way about them. So if God has given you the precious gift of faith, don't settle for a lukewarm love for Jesus. Don't be content with a short five-minute Bible-reading every day and a quick prayer before meals. Protect that little spark of faith and fan it into flame. Cultivate the gift God's given you so that it grows into a radiant, all-consuming, roaring fire. God is with you every moment, so practice paying attention to his presence and delighting in his closeness. Search hard for his majesty in the pages of your Bible. Pray, pray, and pray some more, listening for his precious voice. Look for his beauty in creation. Ask him to show you his glory. *He's waiting to show you who he really is.* And the more you see who he is and personally experience his abundant love for you, the more your love for him will just keep growing. And then, like Mary, you won't be able to hold yourself back from joyfully

---

2. Chester, *Enjoying God*, 21

pouring out everything for Jesus. Like Mary, you'll live a life that's full to the brim with glorious, heart-bursting love for Jesus.

Reflect and respond

1. *What is distracting you from Jesus? Think about what you invest most of your time and attention and emotional energy into.*
2. *What do you need to cut out of your life so that you can make space to cultivate a deep, overflowing love for Jesus?*
3. *What three practical steps can you take this week to spend more quality time with Jesus?*

Pastor A. W. Tozer wrote a wonderful book in 1948 called The Pursuit of God. *It's a passionate call to chase after God with our whole hearts and lives. Today's prayer is paraphrased from Tozer's book:*

O God,
I've tasted your goodness, and it has both satisfied me and made me thirsty for more.
I know how desperately I need more grace.
I'm ashamed that my desire for you is so weak.
O God, I want to want you;
I long to be filled with more longing for you;
I thirst to be made even more thirsty for you.
Show me your glory, so that so I can really know you.
In your mercy, start a new work of love deep inside me.
Woo my soul with the tender words of a lover.
Then give me grace to follow you and leave behind this lukewarm faith that I had settled for.

In Jesus' name,
Amen.[3]

---

3. Tozer, *Pursuit of God*, 26

Meditation verse for the day:

You make known to me the path of life;
in your presence there is fullness of joy;
at your right hand are pleasures forevermore.
(Psalm 16:11, ESV)

Day 37

The Last Supper

(READ MARK 14:12–26)

Passover

JESUS IS IN JERUSALEM celebrating the Passover, just like he's done every year of his entire life. It's not a coincidence that he's going to die in Jerusalem during the biggest festival of the year. Almost 1500 years of Jewish history have been leading up to this exact point. It all started back in Exodus 12 at the very first Passover, when the blood of spotless lambs saved the enslaved Israelites from God's angel of death. The Passover lambs died so that the people could live. This incredible rescue became what the Israelites built their ethnic identity around. It shaped how they saw themselves and how they understood God. It was the most important story in their history; they sang songs about it and taught it to their children and retold the story every year. Bible scholar Tom Wright beautifully describes it as "the Story above all stories for the Jewish people... which all first-century Jews would have known in their bones."[1] Their annual Passover festival was a way of making sure each new generation didn't forget God's salvation in the past.

But the story of Passover was also a symbol, pointing to the way God would save his people in the future, through the Messiah. The Passover happened as foreshadowing, to prepare our imaginations for Jesus. Just like

---

1. Wright, *Simply Jesus*, 65.

the spotless lambs at Passover, the Messiah was going to be sacrificed in our place. His blood would cover over our sins and save us from God's judgment. The Passover was a signpost, pointing to the world-wide salvation story that would happen through the Messiah. So here Jesus sits, at the Passover meal with his closest friends, eating the traditional meal of lamb and flat bread, and singing familiar hymns. But he is about to become the actual Passover lamb. His blood is about to be spilled so that ours doesn't have to be. He's about to become the sacrifice to take our place and save us. He's about to die to set humanity free from slavery to sin, the real eternal Exodus. He is the salvation of God in human form!

Communion

In verses 22–24, Jesus passes bread and wine around the table to his disciples, calling it his body and his blood. We remember this moment every time we celebrate communion. Jesus isn't saying here that the bread is literally his body. He's encouraging us to look at that piece of communion bread and let it remind us of what his body went through for us. He's asking us to drink the communion wine and reflect on the blood he spilled in our place. Jesus is taking things that originally point back to the Exodus story, and explaining that they actually point to him. They're now symbols of a new covenant, the celebration of an eternal salvation story. These Passover symbols used to mean, "God saved Israel!," but they now also mean, "God saved humanity!" Jesus is saying here that we should never, ever forget what happened in Jerusalem that Passover weekend, because it changed everything.

So next time you're receiving communion, don't just rush through it. Christians celebrate communion together for the same reason that Jewish and Christian people celebrate the Passover. Communion reminds us who our God is: a compassionate Father who sacrificed everything to bring us home. It reminds us who we are: beloved children redeemed at a horrific price. The cross is our Story of stories, the story that's in our bones. It's the story we sing about and celebrate with our friends and teach our children. It's the event that shapes our identity, and the foundation of our lives and our hope and our gratitude and our security. Jesus Christ is the Lamb of God who takes away the sins of the world!

If you want to learn more about how the first Passover and the Israelites' exodus from Egypt points us to Jesus over and over again, I recommend pastor Tim Chester's really helpful Bible study, *Exodus For You*.

The Last Supper

Reflect and respond

1. How will today's passage influence how you celebrate communion?
2. Jesus' death and resurrection is the great salvation story of all humanity. What steps can you take to make sure it's the story that shapes your life more than any other story? How can you get it into your bones?

God my Redeemer,
Thank you for the wonder of salvation!
I was a slave to sin, but you paid the heavy price to set me free.
You sent your beloved Son to take my punishment, so that I could have peace with you.
He was crushed so that I could be healed.
His blood was spilled so that mine didn't have to be.
This is my story!
This is who I am.
I am forgiven and free.
I am loved with an everlasting love.
I am yours.
Thank you.

In Jesus' name,
Amen

Meditation verse for the day:

"Look, the Lamb of God,
who takes away the sin of the world!"
(John 1:29)

Day 38

Jesus Arrested

(READ MARK 14:27–52)

Our suffering Savior

THIS IS A HEAVY passage. Jesus is entering into the hardest time of his life. He's being weighed down with a sadness that's almost too much for him to bear. His closest friends abandon him right when he needs them most. This is a scene filled with desolation and sorrow and loneliness, emotions we don't normally associate with the Son of God. But these are very real emotions that every single human will experience at some point. We all go through times of fear and sadness. We all go through seasons where we feel completely alone. And we all have moments (or days, or years) where we wonder if we have the strength to make it through the suffering ahead. The Bible makes it clear that even though Jesus is completely God, he's also completely human, experiencing all the hardships of life that every other human goes through. This is why Hebrews 4:14–16 is so incredibly encouraging to us:

> "Therefore, since we have a great high priest who has ascended into heaven, Jesus the Son of God, let us hold firmly to the faith we profess. For we do not have a high priest who is unable to empathize with our weaknesses, but we have one who has been tempted in every way, just as we are—yet he did not sin. Let us

then approach God's throne of grace with confidence, so that we may receive mercy and find grace to help us in our time of need."

No matter what you're struggling with today, Jesus understands because he's been there himself. He has personally felt suffocating darkness and despair. He's felt devastating loneliness and bitter disappointment. He's been tempted to just give up and run away. He knows exactly how you feel, and his heart is overflowing with loving compassion towards you in your struggle. And there's more: He's up in heaven right this moment, acting as a high priest on your behalf. That means he's interceding and advocating for you, passionately crying out in your defence before the throne of God. Picture him right now, deeply feeling your pain and praying non-stop for you with all his heart! *This* is what gives us the confidence to pray boldly to the God of heaven. *This* is why we can trust God to respond with mercy and grace to help us when we're feeling lost in our sadness or overwhelmed by our sin. Thank you Jesus!

Prayer in the garden

Jesus is standing on the very edge of the greatest suffering anyone has ever experienced. He's not just going to die a painful death. God's terrible punishment on all the disgusting sins of billions of humans is about to pour out on him. This level of spiritual suffering is unimaginable to us. So what does Jesus do? Pray. And pray, and pray some more. Verse 37 tells us that the first time he prays is for an hour, and after that he keeps praying two more times! When Jesus asks for the cup to be taken from him, he's begging God to free him from his mission, to make a way out for him. He doesn't want to go through with the plan, and he's totally honest with God about that! Just like Jesus, we can always tell God exactly what's on our hearts. God wants us to be open and honest with him. He wants us to bring our whole selves to him in prayer; all our fears and hopes and shame and longings and temptations. He invites us to tell him what we really think, just like Jesus did.

But in spite of how Jesus feels or what he wants to happen, he always ends with the words he taught his disciples in the Lord's prayer: "Your will be done." These words mean, "Father, I've told you what I want. But I trust you. Do whatever you want. I believe your way really is the best way." It's impossible to put into words how radically life-changing this prayer is. Pastor John Onwuchekwa says:

> Jesus helps us see that we must surrender our hearts, and surrendering our hearts takes persistence. Gethsemane shows us that Jesus didn't just utter these twenty-three words only once and then get up and go on his mission. He repeated this request over and over. Jesus spent an hour "saying the same words" (Mark 14:39). He was persistent. . . Jesus wrestles in prayer. He surrenders his heart to God, and he experiences unimaginable strength to move forward (see Luke 22:43). Through his example, Jesus reminds us that surrendering our hearts to God is the pathway to strengthening our hands."[1]

Jesus knows that if God has his way, he will suffer and die. He prays for God's will anyway. This is how he fully surrenders his heart to God: "Your will be done." These are really, really hard words. They don't come quickly or easily. They don't come without an intense spiritual battle. We can't mean them if we're still trying to be in control of our own lives. We can't mean them unless we really trust that our heavenly Father is wise and loving. We can't mean them unless we've personally tasted and seen God's goodness. We can't mean them unless we know God's promises and truly believe that he will faithfully keep every single one of them.

Praying for God's will to be done means trusting that God knows what he's doing no matter what happens. And like Onwuchekwa says, when we fully surrender our hearts and our wills to God, he'll strengthen us to face what comes next. He might not give us the answer we want, but he will *always* give us the grace we need for the next step. The parallel version of this event in Luke 22:43 includes a wonderful detail. In response to Jesus' first prayer, God sends him an angel to strengthen him. So God's answer to Jesus' desperate prayer is: "No, I won't take the cup away. You need to go through with our plan. But you won't face this horror alone. Here's my angel to comfort you, to encourage you, and to strengthen you so that you can persevere in obedience, all the way to the bitter end." Watch Jesus closely as you read over the next few days. You'll notice that once he gets up from these hours of desperate prayer, his sorrow and despair are gone. He's not weak anymore. All the way to the cross, Jesus is calm and focused. When he speaks, it's in a voice of quiet, confident authority. He surrenders his will to his Father in the garden of Gethsemane, and God graciously strengthens him to see his mission through.

---

1. Onwuchekwa, *Prayer*, 72–73.

The disciples abandon Jesus

Peter and James and John are Jesus' closest friends, and they've all told him they want to suffer along with him. But when his deepest crisis comes, not one of them stays awake to support him. Luke's Gospel tells us they fell asleep because they were exhausted by their sorrow. They're overwhelmed with their sadness, just like Jesus is. They're confused and anxious, not knowing what's going to happen next. Jesus shows that the best way to face these emotions is to take them to God in prayer. In verse 38 he tells them they should pray too, as a way of fighting against temptation. Jesus knows they're about to be tempted to give in to fear, tempted to run away. He knows they're going to be tempted to give up on their mission, just like he is. He knows the disciples need to be spiritually prepared for when things get really bad. He knows their lives are about to be in danger, and they'll need God's own strength to get through it. But they fall asleep instead of praying. They miss the opportunity to prepare their hearts to fight fear well. They sleep through their chance to depend on God. And what happens when the temptation comes to run away in fear? The disciples all abandon Jesus. They leave him to face his arrest alone. Onwuchekwa writes, "Jesus' faithfulness to do God's task is directly tied to his prayer. The disciples' faithlessness is directly tied to their prayerlessness."[2] Jesus prayed and God empowered him to persevere through the suffering ahead. The disciples didn't pray, and then they were overwhelmed by their fear.

Reflect and respond

1. *How does Hebrews 4:14–16 encourage you?*
2. *When is praying, "Your will be done," most difficult for you? Why do you struggle to trust God in that area of your life?*
3. *What has the Holy Spirit taught you about prayer through this passage?*

---

2. Onwuchekwa, *Prayer*, 75

Today's prayer is the Lord's Prayer from Matthew 6:9–13, in The Message Bible:

"Our Father in heaven,
Reveal who you are.
Set the world right;
Do what's best –
As above, so below.
Keep us alive with three square meals.
Keep us forgiven with you and forgiving others.
Keep us safe from ourselves and the Devil.
You're in charge!
You can do anything you want!
You're ablaze in beauty!
Yes. Yes. Yes."

Meditation verse for the day:

"*Abba*, Father," he said, "everything is possible for you.
Take this cup from me.
Yet not what I will, but what you will."
(Mark 14:36)

Day 39

Peter Disowns Jesus

(Read Mark 14:53-72)

Peter fails

Simon Peter is having an awful night. First, Jesus prophesies that Peter will disown him three times before the night is through. Peter's probably spent the whole night desperately anxious about what that means. Then, in the garden of Gethsemane, Peter falls asleep while Jesus is praying. Jesus is so disappointed that he singles Peter out of the other sleeping disciples: "Simon, you're sleeping too? *Even you?* You couldn't last an hour with me?" Then in the darkness Peter sees one of his own closest friends coming with soldiers to betray their beloved rabbi. He must have been absolutely devastated in that moment, as the truth about Judas dawned on him. Peter is so determined to protect Jesus, that he draws his sword and cuts the ear off Malchus, a servant of the high priest (John 18:10). But instead of appreciating his help, Jesus tells him off and heals the man's ear! Peter just can't seem to do the right thing tonight no matter how hard he tries. Along with all the other disciples, Peter ends up turning and running, saving himself but leaving Jesus alone and surrounded by armed men. Finally, around the fire in the high priest's courtyard, Peter loudly denies even knowing Jesus. All this on the very same night he'd publicly promised to die for Jesus. Can you imagine how Peter—the loud, confident, passionate leader of the other disciples—felt after a night like this? He must have felt like an absolute failure. He'd betrayed Jesus almost as badly as Judas had.

The hard truth Peter had to face is that his love for Jesus wasn't actually as strong as he thought it was. The loyalty he staked his life on evaporated. The faith he thought was rock-solid failed as soon as things got too hard. When the temptation to run away from danger came, he gave in almost straight away. Like Peter, when life's good we tend to think we're stronger spiritually than we really are. But we *all* fail sometimes. In big ways and in little ways, just like Peter did. We give in to a temptation we never thought would trip us up. We fall back into old habits that we thought we had grown out of. We say something we're completely ashamed of. We let our fears overwhelm us. We act like we don't belong to Jesus. We choose security and safety over being with him.

Failing can be absolutely devastating. But failure can also be a mercy, because failure can help us see ourselves clearly. Our failures strip away our self-confidence and our pride. Our failures show us our weaknesses, and remind us that all our strength comes from Jesus alone. Our failures can bring us to our knees before the throne of God, which is actually the very best place to be. Failure hurts, but it can also be the first step towards deep spiritual growth, if it leads us to depend on ourselves less and depend on God more. Knowing how weak we really are is a gift from God, because God's power is displayed most magnificently in the lives of humble, weak people.

The grace of Jesus

The best part of this story is Jesus' faithfulness to Peter. Even though Peter has disappointed him and denied him and abandoned him, Jesus never gives up on Peter. Jesus never turns his back on Peter. In fact, he just keeps showing Peter love and forgiveness. If we jump ahead in the story to after Jesus' death and resurrection, we see that Jesus even graciously gives Peter a chance to redeem himself. Soon after he is raised from the dead, Jesus meets Simon Peter and a few other disciples while they're out fishing (John 21:15–17). As they eat breakfast together on the beach, Jesus asks Peter the same question three times in a row: "Simon, do you love me?" He's deliberately giving Peter three opportunities to publicly affirm his love, after his three denials. He offers to let Peter try again. Jesus invites Peter to follow him again and to lead his people. He's welcoming him back. He's giving him another chance. And that's the thing about Jesus: he *always* gives us another chance.

The book of Acts tells us that within a few weeks of Jesus going back to heaven, Peter was a transformed man. He wasn't suddenly perfect, but he was filled with the Holy Spirit, and he boldly preached about Jesus to anyone who would listen. His very first sermon led three thousand people to believe in Jesus! He was arrested and threatened with death for Jesus' sake, but this time he stood firm and confident and joyful in his faith. For many decades, Peter was one of the greatest leaders of the first Christian churches. And eventually he gave his life for his beloved Jesus Christ, just like he'd promised to do so many years before. In his grace, God allowed Peter to finally keep the vow he'd made on that awful night when Jesus was arrested.

God of restoration

Peter's testimony reminds us that our failures don't define us. We are not the worst thing we've ever done. In Jesus, we always have a fresh start. Before the beginning of creation, when Jesus chose you to be his, he already knew all the ways you'd fail him. He knew exactly how weak you are. But he chose you anyway. He still loved you. He still died for you. He still gives you the gift of his Spirit. Nothing you've ever done has surprised him. And nothing you could ever do will destroy his love for you. He doesn't only love some improved future version of you, and he's not waiting for you to become spiritually mature before he loves you fully. He loves the very worst version of you, with all his heart. Even when you're at your very worst, he couldn't love you any more.

Our God rebuilds the broken and strengthens the weak. He saves the lost and forgives the sinners. He's a God who loves to give his strength to the weak. He throws parties for prodigal sons and daughters who come home. Because if you're his child, the end of your story is eternal glory in Christ Jesus. God himself will keep you and make sure you get there. Your failures don't get the last word in your story, *God does.* So if you've failed God today, don't lose heart. Let go of your pride and let your failure humble you. Repent and turn back to the loving God who's waiting to forgive you and refresh your soul. Let him graciously restore you. Depend on him, and see how he delights in being faithful to you. Pray for the Holy Spirit to strengthen your faith, so that you don't fall for the devil's temptations again. You are God's child, and he won't ever let you go. He's growing something holy in you, and he *will* finish what he started in you. The end of your story is glory. The end of your story is heaven. Hallelujah!

Reflect and respond

1. Think of a recent time you failed God in some way. What does that failure show you about yourself?
2. What does Peter's story teach you about the character of God?

Faithful Father,
I'm just like Peter; I fail you over and over again every day.
I give in to temptations that lead me away from you.
I give in to fears instead of trusting you.
Forgive me.
Thank you for your faithfulness to me.
Thank you that you delight in restoring my soul and healing my wounds.
Thank you that you love to forgive.
Holy Spirit, please strengthen my faith and empower me to stand firm against the attacks of the devil.
I want to be faithful to you.

In Jesus' name,
Amen.

Meditation verse for the day:

For this is what the Sovereign Lord says:
I myself will search for my sheep and look after them…
I will search for the lost and bring back the strays.
I will bind up the injured and strengthen the weak.
(Ezekiel 34:11, 16)

Day 40

King of the Jews

(READ MARK 15:1-20)

ONE PHRASE IS REPEATED over and over again in this devastating passage: "King of the Jews." Jesus is on trial, accused of calling himself the king of the Jews. It's enough to get him executed. It's enough to turn the crowds against him, only days after they'd cheered for him as he entered Jerusalem on a donkey. But what was so bad about being called the king of the Jews? Why did that make people hate him so much? It can be really hard for us to understand what's going on here, unless we try to put ourselves in the shoes of the first century Jewish community Jesus was part of.

The promised Messiah

For almost 1500 years, ever since the Passover and the exodus from Egypt, God's people had been waiting for the promised Messiah. Their scriptures (the Old Testament) were filled with wonderful prophecies about a great Rescuer who was coming to lead his people. Jewish people knew that God would eventually keep his promise, and every new generation desperately hoped that this Christ (which is the Greek word for *Messiah)* would come soon. They thought he would be the king who would finally bring them the peace they longed for. They believed he would set them free from the evil empires who were oppressing and enslaving them. They thought he would rebuild their temple in all its former glory, and bring the Jewish people great honor. The Gospels all show us how much this promised king was at the front of everyone's minds, even after so many centuries of waiting. John's Gospel says the first few disciples to follow Jesus race to tell each other: "We've found the Messiah! It's really him this time! The one Moses and our prophets wrote about is finally here!" (John 1:41). It's hard to imagine their excitement at being part of the moment in history their ancestors had all been longing for!

Not the king they wanted

But all through Jesus' three years of public ministry, there's a disconnect between what the people expect from the Christ and what he's actually there to do. Even his own disciples keep misunderstanding his mission. On their walk into Jerusalem they argued about who would be greatest in Jesus' kingdom, so they're clearly expecting that he's about to make his big move and take his rightful place as king. The thrilled crowds that lined the streets to celebrate as Jesus rode into Jerusalem just a week before must have been on the edge of their seats, waiting to see how he would finally lead the revolution that would overthrow the Romans and free their people.

But Jesus wasn't what they were hoping for. He didn't fit their expectations of who the Messiah would be. As pastor Tim Keller says, "Throughout Jesus' life, the apostles and the disciples keep saying to him, "Jesus, when are you going to take power and save the world?" Jesus keeps saying, "You don't understand. I'm going to lose all my power and die—to save the world."[1] So when Jesus was arrested, they must have been filled with despair. When he didn't launch an attack on the Romans, they must have felt like he'd utterly failed them. When he didn't even speak up to defend himself during his trials, they must have been bitterly disappointed. It's easy to see why all the disciples abandoned him; this is the opposite of everything they'd hoped for. It's easy to understand the rage of the crowds; they must have felt like Jesus had lied to them, getting their hopes up for nothing. How dare this weak, ordinary man claim to be God's Anointed One? Who does he think he is? The true Messiah would never surrender to the hated Romans without a fight! They were so heartbroken and angry that they felt Jesus deserved to die. The huge tragedy here is that so many of the exact people who had been waiting for God's Messiah missed him when he was right in front of them. They were looking in the wrong direction. They were longing for a king on a throne, so they didn't recognize him when he showed up on a cross instead.

---

1. Keller, *Hidden Christmas*, 77.

Jesus your King

You might have the same doubts today as many of the people around Jesus. Maybe you wonder how a Middle Eastern carpenter from thousands of years ago could really be your king today. Jesus of Nazareth is the fully human Jewish man who died on a cross over two thousand years ago. But Jesus is *also* the eternal Son of God who is sitting right now on the throne of heaven with God. So don't be confused by his humility as he heads to the cross. *Jesus is still the King.* And he's actually the exact kind of king we need most. Two thousand years ago, he came to earth in love and forgiveness, offering reconciliation with God through his own death. Right now, we're living in a window of time between the cross and the Judgment Day, when it's our last chance to swear our allegiance to King Jesus. This is still the time of the Lord's favor, when all people have the opportunity to repent and be saved. The offer is still open. But one day—maybe very soon—it will be too late. Because the next time God's Son comes back, there will be absolutely nothing meek and gentle about it.

At the very end of the Bible, John writes about his vision of Jesus the King when he returns to earth at the end of time:

> "Then I saw Heaven open wide—and oh! a white horse and its Rider. The Rider, named Faithful and True, judges and makes war in pure righteousness. His eyes are a blaze of fire, on his head many crowns. . . The armies of Heaven, mounted on white horses and dressed in dazzling white linen, follow him. A sharp sword comes out of his mouth so he can subdue the nations, then rule them with a rod of iron. He treads the winepress of the raging wrath of God, the Sovereign-Strong. On his robe and thigh is written, KING OF KINGS, LORD OF LORDS" (Revelation 19:11–16, MSG).

Jesus of Nazareth, the humble rabbi who is being whipped and mocked and spat on, is also the eternal King of kings and Lord of lords. Right now he is the Lamb who was slain, but he will come back as the Lion of Judah. And when he comes, riding on the clouds, all the world will know it. No one will ever be able to deny that he is the King again. Every knee will be forced to bow before him.

You can trust him

It can be scary to give Jesus kingship over our lives. Jesus makes it clear over and over again that following him will cost us everything. He tells us that life in God's kingdom means dying to ourselves, carrying our cross and following him anywhere, even into great suffering. It means becoming a servant, obediently following our King wherever he leads us. All of this is *hard*. It's actually so hard that it's humanly impossible, unless God's Spirit transforms our desires from the inside out. So how do any of us learn to trust God enough to let him sit on the throne in our hearts? How do we learn to joyfully surrender every part of who we are to him?

My best advice is to focus your heart and mind on the gospel of Jesus Christ, day in and day out. Fix your eyes on Jesus' sacrifice for you. Meditate every day on how much he gave up to bring you home. Soak your imagination in his mercy towards you. Reflect on the horrific price he paid on the cross to cover your sins. And as you see his love for you more clearly, your trust in him will grow deeper and deeper. The king you're surrendering to is not a violent dictator interested in bossing people around. Your King is a Shepherd who lays down his life for his sheep. Your King is a joyful Father who celebrates the return of every rebellious child. Your King is a servant who kneels down and washes your dirty feet. He's the King who went to hell in your place. He is worthy of all your trust. He wants your eternal happiness even more than you do, and he's the only one who can lead you on the right path to find it. Surrender everything to him. Let him sit on the throne in your life. Anything he asks you to give up along the way isn't necessary for your eternal happiness. And he's promised to provide every single thing that is. Trust him.

Reflect and respond

1. *What do you expect from Jesus? Is it possible that you're missing out on experiencing his love and peace and joy because he's a different kind of Savior than you're hoping for?*
2. *Does thinking about the second coming of Jesus the King change how you live your life and relate to the people around you? How? Why?*

My Lord and my God,
You are the Rescuer who came to find me before I even knew I was lost.
You are the Savior who gave your life to give me life.
I don't have the words to thank you.
I want you to be the King over all of my life.
I trust you. Help me trust you more.
Help me see your love more clearly.
I want my whole life to honor Jesus my King.

In Jesus' name,
Amen

Meditation verse for the day:

Again the high priest asked him,
"Are you the Messiah, the Son of the Blessed One?"
"I am," said Jesus. "And you will see the Son of Man
sitting at the right hand of the Mighty One
and coming on the clouds of heaven."
(Mark 14:61–62)

Day 41

The Death of Jesus

(Read Mark 15:21–41)

If you've heard the crucifixion story lots of times, it can be easy to read this passage quickly without thinking about the full meaning of it. As uncomfortable as it can be to meditate on the death of Jesus, the cross is actually at the very heart of our Christian faith. It's the main event that everything else has been leading up to and preparing for. Jesus on the cross for us is *the gospel, the good news*. This is the event that changed all of history, that breaks the power of sin in our lives, and that transforms our lives now and into eternity. It's the deepest reality behind everything else in the universe. It's the truest truth about who you are as a child of God.

So take a moment to pray. Humbly ask God's Spirit to give you a fresh wonder at the message of the cross, and a deeper understanding of what Jesus' death means for you. After you've prayed, read this passage again—slowly. Picture what's happening to Jesus, and remember that everything he does is out of love for *you*, taking *your* place. Bow your heart in awe and gratitude before Jesus' passionate, selfless love for you. Reflect on how deathly serious your sin is, that this is the price Jesus had to pay for it. This is the most important event in human history. This is the moment Jesus finishes everything that needed to be done to make peace between us and God.

The Death of Jesus

The cosmic cross

We can *almost* wrap our minds around the physical agony Jesus is in. We can try to imagine the pain of the huge nails, his bloody back whipped raw, the thorny crown pressed down hard, and the horror of slowly suffocating to death. We can guess that his heart was breaking as he looked down from the cross at his distraught mother, who had to stand there helplessly and listen to the crowds mock him and laugh at his pain.

But Jesus' physical death is only part of the story. He wasn't just another martyr killed for his beliefs. On the cross, two layers of things are happening at the same time. On one level, Jesus the man dies painfully. That's awful enough. But on a deeper spiritual level, unseen by human eyes, something cosmic is also happening. This is the history-shaking, eternity-shaping moment the Son of God lays down his life as a substitute for sinners. He personally pays the price for our evil and rebellion, taking God's anger on himself even though he'd done nothing to deserve it. Jesus willingly stands underneath the terrifying wrath of Almighty God as it pours out on him, once and for all. That's why there are three hours of supernatural darkness in verse 33, representing God's judgment and anger toward sin. This is why he cries out on the cross in such desperation, "My God, my God, why have you forsaken me?" Dane Ortlund describes it like this:

> "What *happened* at the cross, for those of us who claim to be its beneficiaries? It is beyond comprehension, of course. A three-year-old cannot comprehend the pain a spouse feels when cheated on. How much less could we comprehend what it meant for God to funnel the cumulative judgment for all the sinfulness of his people down onto one man... What is physical torture compared to the full weight of centuries of cumulative wrath absorption? That mountain of piled-up horrors? ... When communion with God had been one's oxygen, one's meat and drink, throughout one's whole life, without a single moment of interruption by sin—to suddenly bear the unspeakable weight of all our sins? Who could survive that? To lose that depth of communion *was* to die. The great love at the heart of the universe was being rent in two. The world's Light was going out."[1]

The agony Jesus experienced in his spirit is something that no other human being has ever experienced in the history of the world. He suffered under the pain of God's holy anger, and also the pain of being separated

---

1. Ortlund, *Gentle and Lowly*, 199–201.

from the Father he infinitely loved. This is pain we can't even start to understand. Our imaginations just aren't big enough. Jesus literally experienced God's judgment on billions of sinners, all at once.

Without the cross, all our sin would still be ours, and one day we would still need to pay our debt to God. Without the cross, God's just and holy hatred towards sin would crush us. Without the cross, we would never be able to come into God's presence as his beloved children, because our guilt would always come in between us. But on the cross, Jesus the King does for us what we could never do for ourselves. No wonder the cross is such good news!

The gospel for you today

If you have faith in Jesus Christ, what happened on the cross doesn't only change where you go after you die. It also changes every part of your daily life—every thought and feeling and decision and action and word you speak. How? The cross reminds us how deeply God loves us, which gives us abundant peace and joy. The cross reminds us how high the cost of our sin was, which encourages us to run from our sin and run after holiness. The cross reminds us how far God already went to bring us into his family, which gives us confidence that he'll do everything necessary to bring us all the way home to him. The cross reminds us how much we're worth to God, which gives our lives dignity and value that isn't dependent on what others think about us. The cross reminds us there is nothing we can do to save ourselves, which frees us from the striving of trying to be good enough to earn God's love. The cross reminds us that it's God who justified us in Christ Jesus, which gives us security that we can't lose our salvation because we never earned it in the first place. The cross reminds us that God can work wonderful good out of horrific evil, which helps us trust him through the hard times in life. The cross reminds us how much Jesus has loved and forgiven us, which motivates us to love and forgive the people around us. Can you see how a life that's flooded with the gospel looks different? Gospel-saturated people are joyful, grateful, secure, courageous, kind, forgiving, generous people. The cross is the answer everyone's looking for. The cross is the rock to build your life on.

The Death of Jesus

Reflect and respond

1. What does the cross show you about how God feels about you personally?
2. Think of areas of doubt or fear or anger in your life. How could fixing your eyes on the gospel every day bring healing and transformation to those areas of your life?

God of my salvation,
Thank you for the cross.
Thank you for the price you paid to bring me home to you.
Thank you that you are the God who loves to save sinners.
I could never deserve your love, but you love me anyway.
I could never deserve your forgiveness, but you forgive me anyway.
I am amazed by your mercy and grace.
I am overwhelmed by your abundant kindness to me.
May my whole life reflect the beauty and truth of the gospel, through the life-giving, heart-transforming power of your Spirit.
I love you.

In Jesus' name,
Amen

Meditation verse for the day:

But God demonstrates his own love for us in this:
While we were still sinners, Christ died for us.
(Romans 5:8)

Day 42

The Cross of Love

(READ MARK 15:21–38)

SINCE THE CROSS CHANGES *everything*, let's linger over it for a bit longer. Let's slow down and let it infuse deeply into our hearts and minds, so that it can start to shape every single part of our lives. To do that, we're going back in time to Isaiah, who prophesied about the coming Messiah in his four wonderful 'servant songs'. Pastor Tim Chester explains that meditating on the prophecies of Isaiah can help us really see the beauty of what happened on the cross:

> "Though he wrote 800 years before Jesus came, Isaiah gives us such a rich and intimate portrait of the death and resurrection of Jesus. Here, as clearly as almost anywhere else in the Bible, we see the true meaning of what was taking place as Jesus was nailed to the cross. But this section of Isaiah is not simply an explanation. It's a powerful and affecting portrait of the personal cost of our salvation. . . I want our jaws to drop as we stand open-mouthed before the cross, lost for words as we see the love of Christ in all its fullness."[1]

So let's journey back to Isaiah 53 and fix our eyes on the cross. As you savor God's radical, passionate, sacrificial love for you, let your jaw drop open and your heart sing out in gratitude.

---

1. Chester, *Beauty of the Cross*, 7–8.

Isaiah 53:4-5

> "Surely he took up our pain
> and bore our suffering,
> yet we considered him punished by God,
> stricken by him, and afflicted.
> But he was pierced for our transgressions,
> he was crushed for our iniquities;
> the punishment that brought us peace was on him,
> and by his wounds we are healed."
> (Isaiah 53:4–5)

Look at what these verses say should have been ours: pain and suffering. But look at what we got instead: peace and healing! How? Because Jesus took our punishment, our affliction, our piercing, our crushing, our wounds. Everything that happens to Jesus as he dies is completely unjust. He didn't deserve any of it. But you know who did? Human beings. I do, and you do. All of the pain and suffering should be ours. We should be the ones forsaken by God. We should be judged for our guilt. Isaiah makes it really clear here that Jesus was taking *our* place on that cross, and that everything he experienced should have happened to us instead. That would have been justice. But he took our place as our substitute. He was punished so that we don't have to be. Tim Keller describes the moment when Jesus cried out on the cross:

> "Jesus, the Maker of the world, was being unmade. Why? Jesus was experiencing our judgment day. "My God, my God, why have you forsaken me?" It wasn't a rhetorical question. And the answer is: For you, for me, for us. Jesus was forsaken by God so that we would never have to be. The judgment that should have fallen on us fell instead on Jesus."[2]

These verses from Isaiah remind us that the cross is incredibly personal for me and for you. *This is our story.* We should never be able to read about Jesus on the cross without our hearts breaking with grief and gratitude, knowing that it should have been us suffering there instead of him.

Isaiah 53:6

> "We all, like sheep, have gone astray,
> each of us has turned to our own way;

---

2. Keller, *King's Cross*, 202.

and the Lord has laid on him
the iniquity of us all."
(Isaiah 53:6)

Maybe you don't feel like your sins are really all that bad, and wonder why the judgment of God needs to be quite so harsh. Like, surely God should save all the crushing and forsaking for really evil people, right? Not ordinary people like us! But here Isaiah gives us the Bible's definition of sin: *turning to our own way*. Sin is trying to do life on our own terms. Sin is not treating God as God, because we want to be our own gods. We want to live the way *we* think is right.

But why is this so terrible? Why does this deserve such a severe punishment? Because God is the only one who has the right to be God. He is our Creator. Everything we have is a gift from him. We owe him the breath in our lungs. God's also the only one worthy of being God because he's unimaginably different from us. "God does not merely exist in the highest possible category; he goes beyond the concept of categories. He *creates* the categories."³ God has existed for all eternity, he never changes, he's all-powerful, he knows everything there is to know, and he's completely holy, which means that everything he does is perfectly good and right and wise and pure. He has authority over the whole universe. Compare yourself to him for even a moment and it's pretty obvious that you aren't quite on his level, right? It's absurd to say to a God like this, "Thanks, but I got this. I think I can run my life better than you can." All the mess in the world is because billions of us keep stubbornly trying to do things our own way. But this verse tells us that all this mess is exactly what Jesus carried on the cross. It was all counted against him, as if he had personally done it. He was punished for it all.

Isaiah 53:11

"After he has suffered,
he will see the light of life and be satisfied;
by his knowledge my righteous servant will justify many,
and he will bear their iniquities."
(Isaiah 53:11)

---

3. Ramsey, *Truth on Fire*, 27.

Isaiah says here that Jesus' suffering justifies many. Justify is a legal word, so imagine standing in a courtroom before God the Judge. You know that you're definitely guilty of the crime and fully deserve a punishment. Yet the Judge announces that you're completely innocent because of what Jesus has done in your place. You have been justified. This doesn't mean that you weren't actually guilty of the crime in the first place. It doesn't mean your crime wasn't very serious. But it means that if you have faith in Jesus, all your guilt has been officially pardoned, and legally you're now declared to be completely righteous in the eyes of God. God's final verdict over you is, "*Not guilty!*" and nothing in heaven or on earth can change his mind. As Romans 8:33–34 tells us, "Who will bring any charge against those whom God has chosen? It is God who justifies. Who then is the one who condemns? No one." This means that because God has justified you, you can never lose your not-guiltiness. Satan (whose name means 'The Accuser') can never accuse you again. No one can take you back to court and have you tried for your sins again. The case is closed. God himself has done *everything* that needs to be done, and he's made his final decision. Do you treasure this truth, and live every day like it really is true? Knowing that nothing can ever steal us away from God or change his judgment over us can give us incredible freedom and peace.

I think the most stunning part of this verse is that it describes Jesus as "satisfied" with what he did on the cross. After all his horrendous suffering, Jesus looks back on it all and smiles with satisfaction. After going through hell for us, Jesus remembers it with absolutely no regrets. He's happy with his choice. He's fully content with what he's done for us. Even on your very worst day, he looks at you and says, "You were worth it all."

Reflect and respond

1. *What does the cross mean for you personally?*
2. *Isaiah 53:6 describes sin as 'turning to our own way.' How does this challenge how you think about sin in your own life?*
3. *How does it make you feel to know that Jesus is satisfied with the horrific price he paid for you?*

Today's prayer is adapted from parts of Isaiah 53 in The Message translation:

Lord Jesus,
It was my pain you carried—my disfigurement, all the things wrong with me.
It was my sins that did that to you, that ripped and tore and crushed you—my sins!
You took the punishment, and that made me whole.
Through your bruises I get healed.
I'm like a sheep who has wandered off and gotten lost.
I've done my own thing, gone my own way.
And God has piled all my sins, everything I've done wrong, on you.
You were beaten, you were tortured, but you didn't say a word.
You died without a thought for your own welfare, beaten bloody for my sins.
Even though you'd never hurt a soul or said one word that wasn't true.
Still, it's what God had in mind all along, to crush you with pain.
The plan was that you give yourself as an offering for sin so that you'd see life come from it—life, life and more life.
Out of that terrible soul-pain, you saw it was worth it and were glad you did it.
Through what you experienced, you made me righteous.
You yourself carry the burden of my sins.
Thank you, thank you, thank you.

In Jesus' name,
Amen.

Meditation verse for the day:

But he was pierced for our transgressions,
he was crushed for our iniquities;
the punishment that brought us peace was on him,
and by his wounds we are healed.
(Isaiah 53:5)

Day 43

Some Surprising Disciples

(Read Mark 15:39-47)

The centurion

THIS IS A REALLY incredible moment. Jesus has just died. The Roman centurion who's guarding the crosses has been watching everything that's happened. He's probably seen dozens or even hundreds of crucifixions before. But there's something so unique about the way Jesus died, that he's totally convinced Jesus is the Son of God. This enemy of God's people, whose job involves torture and murder, suddenly believes the Jewish peasant man dying in front of him is *God*. This centurion, who has probably spent his life worshipping at least a dozen different Roman gods and goddesses, looks at Jesus' battered body and recognises that he is in the presence of the one true God. It sounds crazy! But this man's story encourages us that anyone, anywhere, can know Jesus. No matter who we are, God can open up our eyes to see him for who he really is. There's nothing about our past or our present that can disqualify us: God loves to welcome undeserving outsiders into his kingdom. God loves to save sinners.

The women

Did you know that Jesus had far more than just twelve disciples? He handpicked twelve men to be his core group, but many times in the Gospels we read that he actually had hundreds of other disciples following him around the countryside. Verses 40 and 41 are very precious, because they give us a little glimpse of just how radically counter-cultural Jesus was. These verses tell us that near the cross, watching Jesus die, were his most faithful disciples: the women. We already know how epically his twelve closest disciples failed him in the hours before the crucifixion, and apart from John we're never told if any of them made it to the cross that day. Perhaps they were still too ashamed or afraid to show their faces. But the women were there. *Lots of women.* Mark wrote most of his book based on Peter's eyewitness testimony, but he lets us know who his sources are for this particular part of the story: Mary Magdelene, Mary the mother of James and Joseph, and Salome. I love Tim Keller's note here:

> "When it comes to the death, burial and resurrection of Jesus, the only followers of Jesus who were with him through all three of those things, are his female followers. . . At the most crucial moment in the history of salvation, God trusts a group of women with the whole story. They're almost the lifeline of the gospel. . . God makes women his witnesses at a time in history in which no other society would have trusted them with the same job."[1]

In Jesus' community, women were not allowed to be legal witnesses. They weren't considered reliable or trustworthy, and their testimony wasn't taken seriously. And yet God chooses *them* to be his eyewitnesses. He trusts *them* with his story. If you read the Bible from beginning to end, it's a theme you'll see over and over: God always chooses to use weak, marginalized people to do his most important work. He never chooses the people we would expect. He loves to show his strength in our weakness. He loves to remind us that he doesn't judge people based on the same things we judge on. That means there's not a single person out there who God can't choose. There isn't a single person who's a write-off in God's eyes. There isn't a single person beyond God's grace.

In fact, Mark isn't the only person to highlight the important role women played at Jesus' death and resurrection. All four Gospel writers take care to note the many women who had financially supported Jesus' ministry, cared for him on his travels, followed him to Jerusalem, and were now witnesses to his death. Author Rebecca McLaughlin has a wonderful book called *Jesus Through the Eyes of Women,* and she writes,

---

1. Keller, "Women, Pagans and Pharisees," 00:04.

Some Surprising Disciples

> "The four New Testament Gospels tell multiple stories of Jesus relating to women. Poor women. Rich women. Sick women. Grieving women. Old women. Young girls. Jewish women. Gentile women. Women known for their sinfulness. Women known for their virtue. Virgins and widows. Prostitutes and prophetesses. Looking through their eyes, we see a man who valued women of all kinds—especially those vilified by others. Indeed, the way Jesus treated women tore up the belief that women are innately inferior to men: a belief that was pervasive in the ancient world. We should not be surprised, therefore, that women have been flocking to Jesus ever since."[2]

Jesus honored the dignity of every woman he met, in a culture where most religious leaders would not even talk to a woman in public. Women felt seen by Jesus, loved by him, and welcomed by him. In his presence, each woman's soul felt its true worth. And so here we see the women at the cross, beautifully honoring Jesus in his death by doing the only thing they could do: bearing witness. Loving him with their presence during his devastating aloneness. Standing by him even though it could have been dangerous for them. Loyal to him even though it seemed like he had failed his mission. This is a beautiful picture of what faithful discipleship looks like. In quietly following and loving Jesus, they've found an unexpected boldness and courage to stand firm even when they don't have any hope left. They know that they are beloved by Jesus, and it's changed everything for them.

The religious leader

In verses 42–46 we discover another surprising follower of Jesus: Joseph of Arimathea. Joseph is a rich and powerful religious leader, belonging to the council that arrested Jesus. John describes him as a secret disciple who was scared of the other religious leaders finding out that he followed Jesus (John 19:38). But after Jesus' death, Joseph has an incredible change of heart! He decides to publicly associate himself with Jesus, plucking up his courage and asking Pilate for Jesus' body. John's Gospel tells us that Joseph's Pharisee friend Nicodemus (another secret disciple) helps him complete the proper Jewish burial customs, and together they lay Jesus' body in Joseph's own tomb. This is a risky move for Joseph and Nicodemus! Right at the moment when it looks like Jesus' movement has failed, they stand up and publicly say they are believers. Right when it is most dangerous to their careers and

---

2. McLaughlin, *Eyes of Women*, 11.

reputations, they admit they are disciples of Jesus. They're putting everything on the line.

So what's changed for these men? Where has this sudden boldness come from? The fact is, when we see Jesus on the cross for us, it changes us. It humbles us to see the horrendous cost of our sin. It takes away our pride. But it also affirms us to see how deeply we're loved by Jesus. That gives us incredible hope and courage! The cross changed Joseph and Nicodemus. Now they're holding their careers more lightly. Now they're choosing to use their influence and power to care for others. Now they're willing to lose everything to honor their rabbi, Jesus. Have you been radically changed by the cross, like Joseph and Nicodemus?

The church

So what do a Roman centurion, a group of women, and some Jewish religious leaders have in common? Absolutely nothing, except for Jesus. That's one of the most wonderful things about following Jesus. Everyone's welcome! Outsiders are invited in, and insiders are invited to risk everything to serve others. Loving Jesus brings us into a diverse world-wide church made up of people from everywhere and anywhere. The cross of Jesus gives us a deep and beautiful connection with people we might not have anything else in common with. And as we follow Jesus together over the years, we see that the gospel brings healing and reconciliation to some very deep and painful divides in our communities. We find that we're now brothers and sisters with people who used to be our enemies. We discover heart-friends among people we never would have even talked to before. We flourish in relationship with other Christians who are also following Jesus wherever he leads. So, no matter who you are today, there's a place for you in God's family. Whether you're a murderer like the Roman centurion, socially marginalized like the female disciples, or rich and powerful like the religious leaders, there's a place for you in the church. You're welcome here.

Reflect and respond

1. *How does the cross humble you, taking away your pride?*
2. *How does the cross affirm you, building you up in boldness and confidence?*
3. *How does the cross free you up to live more radically for Jesus?*

Father, my rescuer,
Thank you for Jesus on the cross.
I want to live like the new creation you've made me!
You've given me a new identity, a new family, and a new purpose.
Holy Spirit, please give me the boldness and courage to live fully for Jesus.
Help me not to worry about what others think of me.
Help me not to put my hope in worldly things like money and power.
May my life be a love song to you.

In Jesus' name,
Amen.

Meditation verse for the day:

…Anyone united with the Messiah
gets a fresh start, is created new.
The old life is gone; a new life emerges!
(2 Corinthians 5:17, MSG)

Day 44

The Resurrected Christ

(Read Mark Chapter 16)

Verses 9–20

Before we get to the main part of this chapter, it's important that we talk about verses 9–20. In most modern Bible translations, these verses include a note that says something like, "Some of the earliest manuscripts do not include 16:9–20." To understand what this means, we need to know a bit about the history of the Bible itself. Like all ancient writings, each book in the Bible was copied down by hand so it could be shared around. Incredibly, over 5800 ancient Greek copies have been discovered so far! That's literally *thousands* more copies than any other text from ancient times. "With the abundance of New Testament sources, modern scholars are able to reconstruct 99 percent of the New Testament with extreme confidence."[1]

Of course, when people are copying things by hand they sometimes make small mistakes. So imagine that an expert is trying to find out what the original Bible said. She has thousands of ancient manuscripts to compare and contrast, and all of them are almost identical. Comparing all these copies makes it really easy to spot random mistakes here and there, because they stand out from all the rest. The trouble here in this passage is that two of the earliest complete copies we have of Mark's book don't include the

---

1. Broocks, *God's Not Dead*, 168.

longer ending, but all the other copies do.² Thankfully our modern Bibles are very clear about where there are uncertainties in translating the original, just like we see here. That honesty and transparency actually helps us know that the Bible translation we're reading is trustworthy.

Today we aren't going to study this last section of Mark 16, but it's reassuring to notice that it doesn't include anything that's any different from the endings of the other three Gospels. So, whether you think it's original or not, it ultimately doesn't change a single thing about the story of Jesus.

Mary Magdelene

As we saw yesterday, Jesus' faithful female disciples are committed to honoring him any way they can. They're the first ones to visit his tomb on Sunday morning after the Sabbath is finished. (The Jewish Sabbath goes from sunset on Friday to sunset on Saturday.) Mark's Gospel ends with the women being extremely afraid at the news of Jesus' resurrection, but the other Gospels fill in the details of what happens next. John tells us that after the women got over their fright they did eventually tell John and Peter, and that Mary Magdalene ran back to the tomb with them. There in the garden near the tomb, she was the very first person to see her beloved rabbi risen from the dead. She's the one told to spread the word. Tim Keller explains why this is such a big deal:

> "Jesus could have easily arranged to make anyone the first messenger. He chose her. And that means Jesus specifically chose a woman, not a man; chose a reformed mental patient, not a pillar of the community; chose one of the support team, not one of the leaders, to be the first Christian. How much clearer can he be? He is saying, "It doesn't matter who you are or what you've done. My salvation is not based on pedigree, it's not based on moral attainments, raw talent, level of effort, or track record. I have not come to call those who are strong, but those who are weak. And I am not mainly your teacher, but your savior. I'm here to save you not by your work, but by my work." And the minute you understand that, the minute you see yourself in Mary Magdalene's place, something will change forever in you."³

---

2. Orr, "Where Does Mark End?"
3. Keller, *Encounters*, 99.

Do you see Jesus' kindness in choosing Mary to be the first disciple to see him risen? Before Jesus, Mary Magdelene had been nothing. She was possessed by seven demons. She was probably an outcast, avoided and feared by her community. Jesus not only healed her, he also welcomed her along on his journey as a beloved disciple. He invited her into a new family. He loved her. And now he honors her by choosing her to be the first person on earth to see the resurrection with her own eyes, and asking her and other women to spread the news to the other disciples. He doesn't do all of this because Mary is especially worthy of his love. She's not. He does all of this because he specifically came to save lost people. He came to be a doctor for anyone who knows they're sick. Mary knows how desperately she needs Jesus. She's eager to receive the free gift he's giving. She's brought all her hurt and shame to Jesus and laid it at his feet. And humble people like Mary are exactly the kind of people God just loves to lavish his goodness on.

Peter

There's another beautifully grace-soaked moment in this scene, in verse 7. It's these two words, spoken by the angel: *"and Peter."* Out of all the disciples, why does the angel single Peter out by name? Think how Peter must have been feeling these past three days. He's grieving the loss of his best friend, and overwhelmed with shame for all the ways he failed Jesus on that last night. He's feeling embarrassed. He's full of regrets. He might not feel worthy to hang out with the rest of the disciples anymore. And yet God's angel goes out of his way to make sure Peter personally knows Jesus wants to see him. *You need to be there too, Peter. He especially wants you to come!* This is stunningly kind. This is grace. Peter doesn't deserve forgiveness. He doesn't deserve to be included in this special invitation. But God shows us his tender, merciful heart in this moment. *And Peter. Don't forget to tell Peter I really, really want him there.*

The heart of God that we see in these two little words is actually the story of the whole Bible. From Genesis to Revelation, the Bible tells the story of a God who goes out of his way to show sinners how eager he is to love and forgive them. He pursues people who have rejected his love, giving them chance after chance to turn back to him. He woos back the unfaithful wife who has cheated on him; he waits with open arms to throw a welcome-back party for the rebellious son who rejected him; he leaves ninety-nine sheep to search everywhere for the missing one. And he says on every page of the Bible that it's all for you: yes, *you*. You're the one whose name is engraved on his hands. You're the one who is precious and honored in his eyes, who he'd give up empires for. You're the one who is specially invited to his wedding feast. You're the apple of his eye. *And you.*

Reflect and respond

1. *How can you practice humbly bringing your weakness and shame to Jesus this week, like Mary Magdelene?*
2. *What does the angel's specific invitation to Peter mean to you? What does it show about God's heart for you personally?*

Today's prayer is based on excerpts from Psalm 25:

God of mercy,
I lift up my soul to you; I give you all of me.
O my God, I trust in you; please save me!
Teach me your ways, lead me in your truth.
You are my only hope; you are my Savior!
Treat me based on your mercy and your love, and not based on how I've sinned against you.
You are good and just, teaching sinners the way to go. Teach me!
You lead humble people in what is right. Lead me!
All your ways overflow with love and faithfulness for those who are your disciples.
Turn to me and be gracious to me, because I'm lonely and struggling.
Look at the mess I'm in and save me from it all!
Guard my soul and rescue me, because I've run to you for help.
You're my only hope, God. I have nothing else.

In Jesus' name,
Amen

Meditation verse for the day:

He won't brush aside the bruised and the hurt
and he won't disregard the small and insignificant,
but he'll steadily and firmly set things right.
(Isaiah 42:3, MSG)

Day 45

Resurrection Life

(Read Mark Chapter 16)

We talk a lot about Jesus dying on the cross to save us from our sins, but it's actually the cross and the resurrection *together* that save us. If Jesus had never been raised from the dead, his death would be just like every other human death in history. Death would have been the end of his story. His resurrection proves that he is who he says he is: the Son of God, and the Savior of the world. His resurrection proves that he actually defeated death. But what does the resurrection mean for us 2000 years later?

Hope for eternity

In 1 Corinthians 15 the Apostle Paul explains that the resurrection promises us eternal life with God. Without the resurrection, this short earthly life would be all we have, so we might as well just live it up before we're gone forever. But because Jesus was raised from the dead, we can have complete confidence that we will also be raised from the dead one day. Because Jesus defeated death, the sting of death is gone for Christians. Death is tragic, but it will not be the end for us. Instead, Jesus' resurrection shows us that something far, far better is waiting for us: the wedding feast of a lifetime! Never-ending life with the God we love, joining together in joy with all of creation! An eternity filled with everything beautiful and true and good, just the way it should always have been. And not only that, but just like Jesus after his resurrection, all Christians will also have an immortal spiritual body of glory and power and splendor. We don't know exactly what these bodies will be like, but we do know that they will be perfected versions of what we have now. Our old bodies will be changed and made new, and then we will live forever with God in the new creation! (If you're interested in diving deeper into the details of life after death, John Piper has a helpful sermon series called 'What Happens When You Die?' which you can access for free online.)

If we really, really believe this promise of eternal resurrection, it *has* to change how we live. Believing this takes away our fear of death or failure or loss, and fills us with hope and confidence and peace about the future. Believing that this life is just the start for us means we don't need to store up our treasures in this world, so we can use everything we have to love our neighbors. We can literally lay down our lives for others, knowing that we aren't really losing anything. We're freed to hold earthly things lightly, which means we're able to let them go easily if God asks us to. When tragedies and disappointments happen, we don't need to despair. We don't need to find our security in our possessions or career or relationships. Disabilities don't need to define us. We don't need to put the weight of all our hopes and dreams on this world. We should be the most free, joyful, generous people ever known! We should be unshakeable! Because there is so much more ahead for us. Much better things than we could even imagine.

Hope for this life

Unfortunately, too many Christians believe that Jesus' resurrection only gives us hope for *after* we die. They think that the resurrection is just good news for our personal spiritual life, but is irrelevant for the things we physically do on this earth every day. Those people are tragically missing out on so much, because the resurrection also offers us hope for right now. Romans 8:20–21 tells us why:

> "Against its will, all creation was subjected to God's curse. But with eager hope, the creation looks forward to the day when it will join God's children in glorious freedom from death and decay." (NLT)

This passage means that the whole created world has been broken by sin. But all of creation is also included in God's resurrection work. He isn't going to start again from scratch; he's going to restore what already exists, setting it gloriously free from sin and death! The resurrection isn't just for God's children, it's for every part of his creation, when "all the broken and dislocated pieces of the universe—people and things, animals and atoms—get properly fixed and fit together in vibrant harmonies" (Colossians 1:20, MSG).

But this wonderful resurrection promise is for even more than just the rainforests and the coral reefs and the endangered animals. Revelation 21:26 says that God will also bring the best parts of human culture and creativity into the new creation where we will live with Jesus for all eternity. The beautiful things we make here on earth for God's glory will somehow continue into eternity, after he makes them perfectly holy and good! Our cultures matter so much to God that he longs to redeem them. This is incredible news. It means that the things we do here can somehow be restored and perfected for all eternity. In the beautiful words of my little son's picture Bible, "one day everything sad will come untrue."[1] Hallelujah!

The promise that all of creation and human culture will also be made new completely transforms our way of thinking about life on this earth. As theologian N. T. Wright joyfully exclaims, "The message of the resurrection is that this world matters!"[2] The environment matters. Cities matter. Music matters. Parenting babies matters. Bakeries matter. Gardening matters. Art matters. Righting injustice matters. Bringing healing to hurting places in our world matters. Advocating for fairness and truth matters. God cares about it *all*. And because it all matters to God, it should all matter to us.

Jesus brought God's kingdom to earth, which means that God's resurrection work has already begun. Redemption is happening all around us, like tiny mustard seeds sprouting deep under the dirt. Starting with the resurrection of Jesus, God is bringing life from death in every part of existence. It's a job that won't be finished until Jesus comes back, but because God is working to reconcile all these things to himself, we should be in the reconciliation business too. This makes a huge difference in our daily lives. It means we should be passionate about partnering in the work of restoration and renewal that God is already doing in his beloved world. We need to take creation care seriously, because our Father does. And because culture matters to God, the wellbeing of our communities should matter to us too. We should spend our lives creating opportunities for the people and animals and places around us to flourish. We should be known for always building other people up, speaking life-giving words, and using our power to empower others. We should be the ones bringing healing and peace and

---

1. Lloyd-Jones, *Jesus Storybook Bible*, 347.
2. Wright, *For All God's Worth*, 65.

justice everywhere we can. We can do this whether we're playing trains with a toddler, working nightshifts at McDonalds, or running a huge company.

Living the resurrection

There are unlimited ways we can participate in God's holy work of restoring and renewing and reconciling. But the beauty of resurrection is that *we can't do it*. Humans simply aren't able to bring life out of death. So the point here isn't that we all need to try harder to fix the broken things in this world. Life with God is never about working more and doing lots of good stuff. The point here is that our powerful God is *already* working resurrection all around us. The point is that that he is *already* lovingly bringing renewal and restoration to every hidden corner of our world. He is quietly moving all of creation and history towards the day when everything sad will finally come untrue. Resurrection is God's work.

Our response is to offer our lives as a useful tool in his hands. He's inviting us to join in with the wondrous redemption story he's already writing in our local community. We don't have control over how things will work out. But we don't need to. Our job is to trust and obey; God's job is to take care of everything else. We received resurrection life as a beautiful gift, and it's a gift that's made for sharing. As we use the skills and gifts and passions God has given us, we will become like a flourishing garden whose springs nourish the deserts around us. As God's Spirit works with his resurrection power inside us, it will naturally overflow out of us as rivers of living water, quenching the thirst of those around us. This is the resurrection life we were made for. This is the life that is truly life!

Reflect and respond

1. *How does the promise of eternal resurrection encourage you to think and live differently?*
2. *How should the promise that creation and culture will be included in the resurrection impact the way you live right now?*
3. *What particular restoring and renewing work is God inviting you to participate in right where you are?*

Resurrection Life

Today's prayer is based on Ephesians 1:17-23:

God of glory,
Please give me spiritual wisdom and insight so that I can know you better.
Open my eyes to see the confident hope you've called me to.
Help me understand the glorious inheritance you have for me as your child.
Give me a vision of the incredible greatness of your power that is already working in me.
I want to know—really know!—the utter extravagance of your resurrection work in me.
You've already given me your Spirit! He lives in me! This means that the same mighty power that you used to raised Jesus from the dead is already in me.
I have everything I need to live boldly and powerfully for you.
Help me trust that this is true, and to live with a confidence and peace and generosity that shows others it's true.
Jesus, you have all authority in heaven and earth, far above any ruler or power or leader who has ever existed in all of creation.
And you have promised to fill me with yourself! To make me whole, and to restore me, and to be everything I need.
Help me stand on this promise and flourish like never before.
I want your streams of living water to flow out of me.
Thank you for inviting me to participate in your beautiful work of reconciling everything in all creation to yourself.
Show me the resurrection work you're calling me to do, right here and now.
Here I am, use me.
Teach me how to live and to love others out of your strength, not out of mine.
I love you.

In Jesus' name,
Amen

Meditation verse for the day:

I also pray that you will understand the incredible greatness of God's power for us who believe him. This is the same mighty power that raised Christ from the dead and seated him in the place of honor at God's right hand in the heavenly realms.
(Ephesians 1:19–20, NLT)

Bibliography

Bailey, Kenneth E. *Jesus Through Middle Eastern Eyes*. Illinois: Intervarsity, 2008.
Broocks, Rice. *God's Not Dead: Evidence for God in an Age of Uncertainty*. Nashville: Thomas Nelson, 2013.
Chester, Tim. *The Beauty of the Cross*. The Good Book Company, 2019.
———. *Enjoying God*. The Good Book Company, 2018.
Comer, John Mark. *The Ruthless Elimination of Hurry*. London: Hodder & Stoughton, 2019.
Crouch, Andy. *Culture Making: Recovering our Creative Calling*. Illinois: InterVarsity, 2008.
Ferguson, Sinclair, B. *Let's Study Mark*. Edinburgh: Banner of Truth, 1999.
Keller, Timothy. *Encounters with Jesus: Unexpected Answers to Life's Biggest Questions*. London: Hodder & Stoughton, 2013.
———. *Hidden Christmas: The Surprising Truth Behind the Birth of Christ*. London: Hodder & Stoughton, 2016.
———. *King's Cross: The Story of the World in the Life of Jesus*. London: Hodder & Stoughton, 2011.
———. "Women, Pagans and Pharisees." Sermon, Gospel in Life, recorded April 1, 2007. Audio recording of sermon, 39:47. https://gospelinlife.com/sermon/women-pagans-and-pharisees.
Lewis, C. S. *Mere Christianity*. London: Harper Collins, 1952.
———. *The Weight of Glory and Other Addresses*. New York: The Macmillan Company, 1949.
Lloyd-Jones, Martyn. *Spiritual Depression: Its Causes and Cures*. Great Britain: Pickering and Inglis, 1965.
Lloyd-Jones, Sally. *The Jesus Storybook Bible*. Michigan: Zonderkidz, 2007.
McLaughlin, Rebecca. *Jesus Through the Eyes of Women*. Texas: Gospel Coalition, 2022.
Onwuchekwa, John. *Prayer: How Praying Together Shapes the Church*. Illinois: Crossway, 2018.
Orr, Peter. "Where Does Mark End? Handling Snakes and Ancient Manuscripts." May 9, 2023. https://www.desiringgod.org/articles/where-does-mark-end.
Ortlund, Dane. *Gentle and Lowly: The Heart of Christ for Sinners and Sufferers*. Illinois: Crossway, 2020.
———. *How Does God Change Us?* Illinois: Crossway, 2021.

Bibliography

Ortlund Jr., Raymond C. *Isaiah: God Saves Sinners*. Edited by R. K. Hughes. Preaching the Word. Illinois: Crossway, 2005.

Peterson, Eugene. *As Kingfishers Catch Fire*. London: Hodder & Stoughton, 2017.

———. *Eat This Book: The Art of Spiritual Reading*. London: Hodder & Stoughton, 2006.

———. *The Jesus Way: A Conversation in Following Jesus*. London: Hodder & Stoughton, 2007.

Platt, David. *Counter Culture: Following Christ in an Anti-Christian Age*. Illinois: Tyndale, 2017.

Ramsey, Adam. *Truth on Fire: Gazing at God Until Your Heart Sings*. Turkey: The Good Book Company. 2021.

Spink, Kathryn. *Mother Teresa: An Authorized Biography*. New York: Harper One, 2011.

Tozer, A. W. *The Pursuit of God*. Chicago: Moody, 2015.

Tyson, Jon. *Beautiful Resistance: The Joy of Conviction in a Culture of Compromise*. Colorado Springs: Multnomah, 2020.

Villodas, Rich. *The Deeply Formed Life*. Colorado: WaterBrook, 2020.

Wright, N. T. *For All God's Worth: True Worship and the Calling of the Church*. Michigan: Eerdmans, 1997.

———. *Simply Jesus*. New York: HarperCollins, 2011.

www.ingramcontent.com/pod-product-compliance
Lightning Source LLC
Chambersburg PA
CBHW070742160426
43192CB00009B/1537